THE MAKING
of a
PREACHER

Being the Warrack Lectures 1942–1943

by
W. M. MACGREGOR

With an Appreciation by
A. J. GOSSIP

The Westminster Press
PHILADELPHIA

CONTENTS

WILLIAM MALCOLM MACGREGOR
M.A., D.D., LL.D.

Born at Glasgow 1861

Died at Edinburgh 1944

Minister of the Gospel at Troon; Renfield, Glasgow;
St. Andrews, Edinburgh

Moderator of the General Assembly 1919

Professor of the New Testament in Trinity College
Glasgow 1919–1935

Principal of the College 1928–1938

Author of

Jesus Christ, the Son of God
Some of God's Ministries
Christian Freedom
Repentance Unto Life
Christ and the Church
For Christ and the Kingdom, etc.

AN APPRECIATION

by A. J. Gossip, *D.D.*
Professor in Glasgow University

WHEN Samuel Johnson died, a man called Hamilton, who knew him well, set down the situation in a shrewd and final sentence — " Johnson is dead; and there is no one left to remind us of him."

W. M. Macgregor also was a unique personality, so original in the whole make-up of his being that, now that he is gone, something has vanished from us which is entirely irreplaceable.

> " As when a kingly cedar, green with boughs,
>   Goes down, with a great shout upon the hills,
>   And leaves a lonesome place against the sky,"

so, for those whose lives touched his in any of his manifold activities, his passing makes a staring gap that must remain empty and blank.

This was a man built upon royal lines. Dr. Norman Maclean, with that felicitous pen of his, summed up a wholehearted tribute in an apt and accurate quotation — " This was the noblest Roman of them all! " Noble! That is, indeed, the right and fitting word.

When one recalls the stately figure, erect and unbowed to the very end, with a distinction, even a majesty, about him that cleared a space around him, and made others in his vicinity look dull and commonplace and drably ordinary; and the finely chiselled and ascetic face, curiously reminiscent of Dante in some of its moods, but only some, and it had many — Macgregor could, and did, for instance, laugh as heartily as any man, with his features puckered up with merriment, and every trace of grave austerity clean gone; and the unforgettable voice, measured, unhurried, and with one plaintive note in it, wistful and haunting as a curlew's cry, which of itself, and apart from what he was saying, clutched at the hearer's heart; and the many dazzling gifts of intellect and speech and soul — this, of a truth, was a great creature of God, nobly planned and fashioned.

As his name betokened, he came, of course, of Highland stock. Yet, superficially, he showed no trace of his ancestry and blood. By nature he was not fiery-hearted and passionate, as the typical Gael is said to be, but notably calm and cool. As a Church leader, for example, he was not swept away by the mood of the moment, nor carried along by the crowd; upon occasion he led a small minority. Yet the years were apt to justify him; and the Church was likely to stand to-morrow where he stood to-day. Again, in speech he had no rushing spate of rapid oratory, but was among the quietest of speakers. Nevertheless the Celt was fundamental and foundational in him. And what we are assured is his people's natural inheritance was certainly his heritage and birthright, this man so gifted with imagination, and vividness of language, and the instinct of worship, and a most lowly reverence in the house of God, and the sense of God's presence everywhere.

I think he was always religious. Certainly he used to speak with gratitude of his father. And that influence ran far back. But, when he was in College here as a student, there opened a new and deeper chapter in his life. As the moving dedication in his first book puts it, " To the dear memory of those two servants and friends of Jesus Christ, Duncan Macgregor, my father, and Alexander Balmain Bruce, through whom to many, and to me also, was disclosed the glory of the Son of God." I wonder if such revelations ever come to any of our students in our classrooms now. If not, may God have mercy on us all!

Inasmuch as his father and brother, two uncles, two cousins, a cousin's son, and I know not how many more, have all been ministers, some of them touching more than local fame, he sprang from a levitical house. In his case, that was perhaps a handicap, as well as an asset. All sorts and conditions of people in the church, and even hanging about its outer precincts, he understood — none better, few so well. But of outsiders his knowledge was not first-hand, and probably neither very definite nor deep. And while he was a delicate scholar, and a tireless reader, avid and eager to the very end, catholic, original, adventurous, constantly making worth-while discoveries in lonely and unvisited spots in literature far off from the beaten tracks, he had, apart from that, really no hobbies. He never, I think, played any game or was interested in any sport, though, even after eighty, he could still outwalk men in their prime in long and gruelling country tramps. The wonderful Gospel, which for him never became weathered by familiarity or dimmed by repetition, but was like the sea in that, at one time, favourite quotation of his from Tintoretto, who, throwing down his brushes in despair, cried out that " it keeps always growing greater, nobody can paint it "; — that Gospel, and his pulpit, and his congregation, and the many calls and interests of the wider Church to which he gave himself so unreckoningly, these claimed him, fascinated him, contented him, eating into the time most men give to their ploys or to their families. To him these things made life, were life. He had it in him to turn into a dozen spheres; and, with a careless ease, win distinction in any one of them he cared to choose. And yet one can't conceive of him except as the preacher, and the scholar, and the churchman that he was.

His was a remarkable ministry, the seeds of which were carried far and wide. Not that he was ever popular in the sense of jostling crowds and a buzzing of excitement round him — which may be religion; and then again may not. In the forenoon his church was full. But in the evening it was a very select company of worshippers that gathered in out of a wide city which prides itself on its discernment in mental and spiritual things. But those who were attracted by his preaching knew, with conviction, that there was none like it anywhere. Once, coming away, I stumbled upon a fellow minister, still dazed and bewildered by the open vision from which he had not yet emerged. At last, breaking his long silence, he exclaimed, " In that one hour I have received an uplift, in the strength of which my own soul will go many days; and, in addition, three whole sermons that rushed in on me as I worshipped, offered me as a gift." All of which was characteristic. What was said was deep and memorable and arresting. But always that kept opening vistas, down which one's own mind could catch glimpses of endless added truths that crowded in on one. This preacher was like a diviner, in whose subtle hands the hazel wand twisted and turned and pointed. And parched, desperate people had but to drive their spades into the hot, dry, arid sand, and there was living water in abundance.

When they were published, these sermons, preached in the first instance to a few wise and discerning folk — for characteristically Macgregor gave his best to the smaller congregation, feeling that while the morning crowd might be there largely from custom and consuetude, the evening handful were likely really to be seeking God, and must be helped and heartened — when, I say, these sermons were published, they made a wide and immediate appeal. For one thing, since Macgregor was a preacher's preacher, they exercised a profound and permanent influence on numbers of his fellow ministers, and that in all kinds of churches, giving them a new ideal and a fresh conception of what preaching means. And, after five and thirty years, they are still as much alive as when first issued; seem indeed to have won a permanent place for themselves in the small circle of religious classics, with Newman's and Robertson of Brighton's and Dean Church's. And little wonder! Scotland is credited with underlining the sermon in its worship, and with a long line of distinguished preachers. Yet, as I judge, in the whole range of Scottish history, there are no printed sermons that can equal two at least of Macgregor's volumes, always excepting A. B. Davidson's. And to run second to that master is honour enough for anyone.

(What is it in them that gives their author such distinction as a preacher? To begin with, these sermons are literature, pieces of finished English. Every phrase in them
has a bite and cutting edge. And all the words are so used
as to seem clean and new and freshly minted. Not one
among them is worn or blurred through much fingering,
and long passing from hand to hand.

No one could meet him, or hear him speak, without being struck by his unerring instinct for the perfect word.
And he made conscience of it. Now and then in the Gospels we are allowed to hear our Lord thinking aloud. Apparently it was not His way to fling down what was in His
mind in the first words that occurred to Him. He used to
pause, and they could hear Him murmuring, " To what
shall I liken it, and with what comparison shall I com-
pare it? " Nor would He proceed until He had found the
metaphor most likely to force home His thought upon
our dullness, making us see and grasp it. The Principal
had something of that same trait, would not accept such
approximations as thrust themselves upon him; but, both
in conversation and in public speech, would, not infre-
quently, pause until he found the one word that alone
could fully serve his purpose. And the feeling in his finger-
tips for that word practically never failed him.

Partly, this must have been a natural gift. But, none
the less, I think he cultivated it with care — like Johnson,
who had, of course, two styles: the one sonorous, rotund,
and not a little pompous; the other simple, straightfor-
ward, nervous English. Not a doubt it was of this latter
that, when asked how he had won it, he explained that
" he had early laid it down as a fixed rule to do his best on

every occasion and in every company, to impart whatever he attempted in the most forcible language he could put it in; and that, by constant practice, and never suffering any careless expression to escape him, or attempting to deliver his thoughts without arranging them in the clearest manner, it became habitual to him " — words which might be set down about Macgregor no less truly.

And from that care of his there flowed not only literary but spiritual results(Leslie Stephen, writing of the eighteenth century, remarks that in those days there were three, and only three, classes of sermons — those that were dull, and those that were duller, and those that were inconceivably dull!)And Bagehot has multitudes in heartfelt unison with him when he declares: " If we are to be dull, surely we will be dull in silence. Do not sermons exist, and are they not a warning to mankind? " Apparently, to many minds, the words " boring " and " sermonic " are exact synonyms.

Oman of Cambridge was convinced, and I agree, that this is largely due to the undistinguished style, the slatternly flat-footed English too common in the pulpit; to that odd notion that religious truth, flung down anyhow, will, of itself, make its impression. Whereas the men who really influence their fellows do so, not only by what they say, but also by how they say it. At the height of the storm many honest journeymen politicians spoke to us, truly enough, but without much result; whereas a speech from Churchill inspired and rallied us — as they said about John Knox, more than five hundred trumpets blustering together in our ears. The things said were much the same. The way of saying it made all the difference.

Or, who can read the story of the Prodigal without a catch in the voice? Yet listen to it as an imbecile called Harwood once set it down, imagining, poor fool, that he was bettering it! Not " I will arise and go to my father "; but " I am determined to go to my dear aged parent, and try to excite his tenderness and compassion for me. I will kneel before him, and accost him in those penitent and pathetic terms, ' Best of parents, I acknowledge myself an ungrateful creature to heaven and to you. Condescend to hire me into your family in the capacity of the meanest slave.' " Stuff such as that will save no souls. And that is what kills many a sermon, and the truths they blur and smudge! In much preaching the great Christian verities fall dully on bored ears, largely because the language used is so opaque, so colourless, so unarresting. But in Macgregor's hands they leapt at one, startlingly vivid, grew thrilling and exciting, came alive.

Further, there was the splendid use made of his vast and multifarious reading; the skill and aptness and felicity of his quotations, — all first-hand and original and quite extraordinarily telling. There are, of course, those who decry quotations in sermons on the ground that they distract the hearer's mind from the main object. Which saying is sufficient in itself to prove that the good men who make it have never a notion how to quote! Macgregor was a master in an art in which, admittedly, many of us blunder; stated his case, and then, with the perfect quotation, drove the nail right home, buried immovably and forever in the wood. Once indeed, in his book on Galatians, *Christian Freedom*, he seems to me to get a little lost among, and jostled by, his motley crowd of witnesses. But, as a rule, how skilled it is, and how it deepens the impression!

But it was his own thinking and experience, lavishly shared with us, that made his sermons what they are. This man was a preacher because he had heard incredibly good news which he could not keep to himself, but had to speak; because he knew Christ intimately, and exulted in this Friend of his of whom he was immeasurably proud. Not seldom during a sermon his face would break into a smile. Sometimes, I think, it was the artist's joy in the right phrase or the perfect quotation. But oftener it was sheer pride in the Gospel that he was preaching, and in the Christ he was proclaiming, and in the wonderful God whom he was seeking to reveal. It was indeed an irresistible Christ he preached, who stormed the heart, whether one would or no. And, as one listened, how could one keep from wondering adoration of a God shown to be so adorable?

And there is this to add. Apparently the human mind has difficulty in holding together, at one and the same time, both sides of a truth. The sovereignty and holiness of God, and His immeasurable love and kindness and self-sacrifice — the generations sway between these two lopsidedly, with most unhappy consequences. Few preachers have taught both of them so adequately as did Macgregor — " The goodness and severity of God." " A just God and a Saviour."

> " Blest be the everlasting God,
>   The Father of our Lord,
>   Be His abounding mercy praised;
>   His majesty adored."

(But what, above all, gave this preacher his power was the patent fact that he was bringing us no carried story, no rumour blown to him from other lives, which he passed on for what it might be worth, but first-hand evidence, what he himself had seen and heard, and known and proved.) His religion had done much for him. He knew it, and was grateful for it, and eager to share it. I am inclined to think that he was not *naturaliter Christianus;* but rather that, without his faith, he would have been a very different personality from what we knew. " The fear of the Lord is clean." That is the type of phrase that rises to the mind as one thinks of the Principal. And yet this clean soul, so remote from what is soiling and vulgar, so contemptuously indifferent to the world, so generous with himself, had, I think, his own fierce spiritual conflict. He never spoke of it. And his calm and reserve hid from others the dust and noise of it. But it was there. He was a deeply religious man, communing with the Master as few do or can. Of his untiringly active mind, constantly at work upon so many things, it is yet strictly true to say

> " For his one thought was God.
> In that one thought he abode.
> Forever in that thought more deeply sinking."

Yet, the disciple whom Jesus loved had a fierce, even a vindictive, temper and crude and heady daydreams, which show through his discipleship enough to make us wonder what manner of man John would have been if he had never met with Christ. So, Dr. Walton, in his affectionate appreciation of Macgregor, concedes that " he had a difficult nature to manage " — a deft phrase and a true one. Apart from Christ, he might have been a proud, even a ruthless, man. Some, I fancy, may have thought that he was proud. If so, they were wrong, though their mistake was not unnatural. For he was a man of moods. And one had to take him as one found him. One day, one hour, human, genial, abundantly friendly and interested, the next he might stand oppressively silent, and looking through one in a disconcerting way that gave one the uncomfortable feeling that one wasn't really there at all! Yet, though it didn't look like it, even then he was attending wholeheartedly. Once, as a lad, I told him a long and involved story of an amazing happening that had befallen me. He looked bored to death, and showed no glimmer of interest: and, as soon as I had finished, without one word of comment, began to talk of something else; with the result that I crept away, feeling small and crushed. Yet forty years later, in a chaffing speech, he recounted the whole incident as I had told it, with every detail filled in with meticulous accuracy. But people didn't know that he was listening, and sometimes were hurt. As Mr. Stewart reminds us in his lifelike little portrait of Macgregor, it was a friend who quoted aptly of him in such moods, " Who can stand before his cold? "

(Again, his mastery of language enabled him to sum up a situation, or a man, in one swift, often devastating, phrase, so final that it stuck, and so striking that it leapt from mouth to mouth.) Yet this is to be added, that a few of such sayings are enough to create a reputation for them, as if they were habitual, which, in Macgregor, they were not, though the possibility of them was always there. He had a horror of sham and meaningless verbiage. And, studying his Testament more carefully than most men do, he found that to be really Christ-like one must be not only kind and forbearing, but also, on occasion, stern and terrible. And, with the Gospels in one's hands, who can deny it, if Christ is really the ideal, and if He Himself was consistently Christ-like, and not merely now and then? So, in Macgregor, it was not ill-will or malice, but an incorrigible honesty that forged those shafts. In fact the people whom he most liked were, perhaps, the likeliest to receive them. Few men, for instance, had so secure a place in his affection as David Hislop. When he delivered what became his noble book *Our Heritage in Public Worship*, the lectures to the College were much more provocative and bellicose and pugnacious than are the printed pages. There was, for example, a full-throated eulogy of the services of the Greek Church, with much derogatory criticism of our own. Moving a vote of thanks, the Principal delightedly praised both the lecturer and his lectures. And then: " But if you ask us to agree with you, David, that is another matter! As often as I worship in a Greek Cathedral, and watch the service being carried through afar off, and but dimly heard, always what occurs to me is this — ' So the veil of the temple has been stitched together again! ' " A single sentence! Yet a long and learned argument lay shattered and in bits, and had to be remodelled.

In reality, Macgregor was slow to criticize, as I know to my cost. Sometimes I used to ask him to worship where a student was conducting the service, and to have a talk with him about it on some later date, guiding and counselling him. But, if he found the service barren, never once could I induce him to speak to the man at all, though these were the cases most in need of help. Apparently, he couldn't bring himself to hurt the lad. Yet he would not modify the ugly truth; and so kept resolutely silent. Once, when I had worried him to speak, he at last grudgingly replied: " There is nothing to say. He wasn't preaching. He was showing off to me." That was the unpardonable sin. Yet, if that were avoided, he was generous in judgment. " How did the service go? " I asked him once. " Full of faults! But they are all curable. I would be quite willing to worship with him statedly. He was preaching Jesus Christ." That was his test. If it were met, then this fine mind, so sensitive to unseemliness in worship, could bear, in a beginner, with much that was gawky and raw and immature.

He himself didn't resent criticism. He didn't like it. Who of us does? He was not easily influenced by it, but held on his own way. Yet I have spoken to him as bluntly as, almost certainly, any man ever did. And it never made a ripple on our happy relationship. In fact, he could laugh heartily at himself, always a good sign. His custom was to preach from notes, but looking his congregation straight in the eyes. Yet, towards the end, he tried dispensing with paper altogether, and asked me how I liked it. I said that he had always read so freely that it made little difference. He replied: " That is a kindly judgment. My brother worshipped with me the other week. His verdict was that, if my preaching ever possessed any good qualities of any kind whatsoever, they were now entirely lost; while nothing had been gained." A preposterous and very brotherlike judgment! But received with immense good-humour, and a kind of delight in its ruthlessness, and a humility that acquiesced in it. And that was typical. For this man never winced under the blows of fate, but met them with a cool and resolute courage. Nor were the knocks that now and then fall to most men in public life allowed to disturb his equanimity. One really foul blow far below the belt, dealt him by an ungenerous spirit, was taken with a half-amused, half-scornful unconcern that was majestic. He was too big to harbour animosities or grudges. Towards one man, and one man alone, did he allow himself to evince a scorn that touched settled dislike. Why that worthy soul awoke it in him I never even began to understand. " He had a difficult nature to manage "; and, for once, the reins broke in his hands.

The fact is that he was a shy man — shyness takes many forms — with all the difficulties which those who are not shy can't understand; and with a deeply affectionate nature breaking through a natural reserve. All through the later years his customary greeting to me was " Well, my dear! " — which, to an old man, from a very old man, is a moving thing. Indeed, so far from being aloof, he had an abnormal personal interest in his fellow-men. He had, of course, like all of us, those who specially appealed to him. The students, for example, felt that it did a man no harm at least to have some Highland blood in him! But no one was lost to him in the press. Never was he known to forget a face, or a name, even after a quite casual meeting. Dazed students, and simple folk lost in the mass of men, with no distinction or originality to catch and hold the eye, have told me incredible, yet well authenticated, tales of his prodigious and Christ-like memory. To give one instance out of many known to me: "Well, John, so you

have come up." Thus he greeted a student on the day of
his arrival. "And how is your sister Margaret? She must
be nineteen by now." "Yes, sir." "And James? He'll be
seventeen? " " Yes, sir, but how do you know? " " Why,
lad! I spent a night in your father's manse when I was
Moderator! " That was fifteen years before; and at a time
when he was visiting numerous manses and parishes every week. Yet each child was remembered down the years
with exactness, and as an individual apart. There is something God-like about that! What a pastor he must have
been! And yet not always and in every way. For this man,
with his affectionate and tenacious memory, could often
express little of what was so clear and vivid in his own
mind. Mr. White, one of his successors at Troon, told me
that when he had Macgregor back, after long years of ab-
sence, as they moved through the streets the visitor recognized everyone afar off, and recalled everything about
them with startling accuracy — the son who went to Can-
ada so many years ago, the daughter who married and settled in Australia, remembered each by name and in detail. Yet, when they came up to these people whom he
knew so intimately, he had often little or nothing to say to
them. So much so that in the Session it was said regret-
fully, " He has forgotten all about us," until Mr. White
told them the facts.

It was not easy for Macgregor to praise a man to his
face. A smile, a pat on the shoulder, a word or two of
thanks, which men prized like a decoration, that often,
that always, if it were truthfully possible; but usually not
much more. Yet, behind a man's back, he was eager in
gratitude and commendation.

Certainly his interest in individuals made him by far the finest Convener of the Highland Committee, since Rainy. For every missionary, office-bearer, and member in the Isles and the far glens was known to him, meant much to him, was an individual, to be individually helped and guided.

And all that went into his preaching, and made it. Especially did the depth and width of his sympathy, and the fierceness of his own spiritual struggle, give him an understanding of all men's religious struggles that was almost uncanny, yet amazingly heartening and helpful. Epictetus tells us that, as they poured out of the classroom, one would say to the other, " You had no right to blab my story to Rufus, as you must have done." " Yours! " so the other answered. " Yours! Why, it was *me* he was describing! " And Rufus, when they told him, smiled. " I was speaking to my own heart," he said.

And, if his sermons were wonderful, what of the prayers, which most people found no less helpful, and some even more? The depth, the insight, the understanding, the power to say the things we ourselves would have liked to say but could not put them into words, and the things further in of which we had never come in sight! How we were led into the secret of the Presence until sometimes, as at a Communion season, a little more, a very little more, and, the thin veil that separates Him from us broken through, Christ would have been visibly there.

When it was rumoured that Macgregor thought of deserting the pulpit for a chair, men, in astonishment, asked,

Why? He replied, with modesty, that he had learned some things from Bruce which he would fain hand on. He was a notable professor, round whom, year by year, there gathered a band of devotees, to whom his room and personality and teaching were the soul and inspiration of the College. It was fine lecturing that went straight to the heart of things, and that taught what really mattered.

And then there came the years of retirement, in full vigour, not of body only, but of mind, its cutting edge as sharp as ever, as the Warrack Lectures proved, when they were delivered in a room crowded with old students eager to hear again the well-remembered voice.

So, happily, in this life there was no appendix in small print, with the powers muffled, and the man shrunk to a shadow of himself. This was a life lived out, and a grave thoroughly earned. Working to the last, he was out posting an article, just completed, on Moffatt, when the blow fell; and in a little he was gone — spared the long agony of pain and helplessness through which so many have to reach their hard-won goal. This man walked with God. And he was not. For God took him.

Foster alleges, in one of his essays, that of all the books that we have read, some few, eight or a dozen, have done more for us than all the others put together. And it is no less true that of all the people we have known, some few, eight or a dozen, stand out as major influences in our lives. It is an interesting study to note how books and people come and go into, and out of, their pre-eminence for us; give what they had to give; and then are left behind. But a few hold their places. And the years cannot challenge or unseat them. And in the list of many a one, certainly in mine, secure and unassailable, there stands the name of W. M. Macgregor.

" I do not know," wrote Principal John Cairns to his teacher Sir William Hamilton, " what life, or lives, may lie before me. But I know this, that, to the end of the last of them, I shall bear your mark upon me."

Wherefore, for this gift also, thought out for us by His mind, and put into our hand by His —

" Glory be to the Father, and to the Son, and to the Holy Ghost, as it was in the beginning, is now, and ever shall be, world without end." Amen.

AN IDEAL OF MINISTRY

WHEN, rather against my will, I was appointed to this Lectureship, I recognized how little of profit I could give to students on any matters of technique, and thus felt driven to talk out of a long experience of matters more intimate and personal, which vitally affect the making of a preacher. You are preparing to take a share in that ministry in which Jesus Christ is the Chief Shepherd, and therefore I propose first to speak of His ministry, as we find it exhibited in The Epistle to the Hebrews, since this must be the ideal and pattern of our own.

In this Epistle He is presented as a priest, but a priest of an unusual type. In all lands — pagan and Christian alike — the priest has to play many parts, in sacrifice, mediation, counsel, prediction, but beyond all these, and making them all possible, is his solitary privilege of access into the Divine Presence. In its derivation the word temple means a place cut off: it may be a stately building, or a grove of trees, or an open patch of soil, like the space within a Druid Circle, but since it is set apart for the Divine habitation no unaccredited person would dare to pass the line. Even in Jeremiah (Ch. 30:21) we read, " Who is there that would put his life in jeopardy in approaching to me? " But, in virtue of his office and so long as he observed the appointed ritual, the priest was free to enter that haunted and terrible place, and, by offering on the people's behalf prayers and gifts, he could secure for them by proxy the benefits of a personal approach to the god. Such a vicarious priesthood has in all ages served as a convenient device for masking the laziness or the timidity of those who prefer to keep at a comfortable distance from God, and who willingly hand over the whole management of their religion to the priest, and think little more about it. But to any man of resolute temper such a policy must seem intolerable, since his desire is to come close to God, and actually touch Him, spirit with spirit. Augustine exultantly tells of one occasion when " with the flash of a hurried glance I attained to *That Which Is* " — all obscuring veils being rent asunder. In the same way, it is said of Moses (Num. 12:8), " With him will I speak face to face, and the very likeness of the Lord will he behold," whilst Paul's ambition was " with face unveiled to gaze upon the glory of the Lord, and by this gazing to be changed into His likeness " (II Cor. 3:18). That is the temper of all the spiritually stalwart, who seek for directness of relation with God, and since our author belonged to this company his desire was not for a priest who would transact on his behalf, leaving him outside, but for one who would effectively bring him to the very Presence. His chosen Priest he also calls " the Pioneer of Salvation " (Heb. 2:10), as One who had for us men broken a way through to God, and " the Forerunner " (Ch. 6:20), on whose track all men may freely and hopefully follow. We may well be shy of the title and the office of priest in any purely vicarious sense, but in this animating sense of leadership both title and task should reverently be accepted by us as a part of our obligation to follow in His steps.

This conception of the priest's task is bound up with our author's notions both of the world and of salvation. To him the world appeared as like a temple of two chambers — a spacious vestibule and an inner shrine, the vestibule furnished only with perishable copies and imitations of noble things, whilst the glorious originals are within the shrine. God's universe thus appeared to him as a system of counterparts — of copy and original, of the fugitive and the abiding, of objects and relations as they daily meet our eyes and the same objects in their ideal, as they were designed by God. Even the sublimest objects which our senses can report were to him mere shadows and semblances of the true, each having its heavenly counterpart. The Temple in Jerusalem is described by the chronicler as " exceeding magnifical," and no doubt, according to earthly standards, it was so; but this man refers to it slightingly as a mere " shadow of the heavenly " (Ch. 8:5). The beauties of earth may captivate and even intoxicate our spirits, but there is a glory which excelleth: *si talis Natura formata qualis formatrix!* If created Nature is so wonderful, what of the Creator! This will be recognized at once as the doctrine of Plato, and the eclectic Cicero comes very near to our author when he admits that " on earth we have no solid or express presentation of true law or justice: the best we can attain to is shadows and semblances of these [*umbrae et imagines*]. Would that we were more faithful to these shadows, which at least have been taken from the excellent patterns fashioned by the Truth itself."

This Platonic conception of the world determined for
our author his notion of salvation, which he conceived as
an escape from the unsubstantial and an entrance upon
that which is eternal: salvation is to leave the vestibule,
where triflers and the earthbound walk and chatter, and
to pass within the shrine where God is. Without any
touch of Platonism Peter points in the same direction
when he asserts that " Christ suffered in connection with
sins that He might bring us to God," away from every
meaner entanglement to Him who is the Truth.

This conception of salvation determined for our author what the priest's peculiar task must be; but before
entering on this I should like you to note one point of
real importance. On the pedestal of Newman's statue in
London the inscription runs, " *Ab umbris et imaginibus
in veritatem*," from shadows and semblances to the Truth;
from the passing to the abiding, from the busyness of men
to the rest and perfectness of God. Now the unspoken as-
sumption in these words is that such an escape can be secured only at death, which again is Platonic. From the
Orphics Plato borrowed the grave word-play, " $\sigma\hat{\omega}\mu\alpha$
$\sigma\hat{\eta}\mu\alpha$ $\dot{\epsilon}\sigma\tau\iota\nu$ — the body is a tomb." The soaring spirit of
man must through all his days on earth be clogged and
burdened by the flesh, and it is only when death has cut
the detaining cords that the soul can rise to the full enjoyment of the Divine. But our author, Platonist as he was,
had learned in his Christian experience that even before
death it is possible to enter the region of reality. Men are
living here on the frontier of two orders, and at any moment, even in this life, the frontier may be crossed and
they may taste the powers of the world to come. He is

confident that " a rest remaineth for the people of God "
(Heb. 4:9) — a blessing reserved for the future; but with
no less of confidence he affirms that " we who have believed do enter into that rest " (v. 3). There is only one
step to take, one door to open, and a man at once may be
at home with God. It is not surprising then that with such
eagerness he exhorts his friends to " labour to enter in "
(v. 11).

Now in a life thus conceived it is obvious what at least
part of the priest's task must be: (he has to awaken unrest
in his fellows, a divine discontent, a craving for something
high and lordly which is being missed, and then he must
lead and assist them towards that goal of their awakened
desire. It is obtrusively the fact that, even if this world
be a passing show, with aims unworthy and joys short-
lived, a mass of people settle down into it with a fair measure of contentment. It may be they are too easily satisfied,
but, as the proverb says, " a bird in the hand is worth two
in the bush," and since higher things are out of reach they
take what comes and make the best of it, remaining deaf
to more ambitious calls. This is the mood of millions of
our countrymen: they are creatures of God's fashioning,
heirs, if they would believe it, of the life everlasting, yet
they scarcely give God a thought. Without any visiting of
self-reproach they remain in the outer vestibule, and it is
here that the priest, as this man conceives him, has to find
them. He has to make them aware of their kingly destiny
and quicken in them a desire after it, and thus he seeks to
bring them to God. On our human level this is our task
also as preachers, so it is wholesome for us to consider the
kind of priest which such a task demands.

1. Our author's first claim is that such a priest must himself be a man with men. He flings out an aphorism (Ch. 2:11) which seemed to him so obvious as to require no demonstration — " He who sanctifies and those who are sanctified are of one group." In strictness of grammar it is possible to read the words also as meaning that both Jesus and His poor clients proceed from the one God, but this is not strikingly relevant, and it is even a little commonplace. So it seems to me better, with some great scholars, to find in the phrase the broad ethical assertion that whoever is to raise the level of his neighbour's existence must make common cause with him, and certainly no more practical precept for us as ministers could be imagined. Good advice, as we bitterly know, may be the most futile of human services, and exhortations delivered with any air of conscious superiority tend at once to exasperate listeners with the suspicion that the man who talks so confidently is taller than themselves only by the height of the pulpit. They feel that if the preacher understood them better his sermons would be shorter and more to the point. Nearly sixty years ago I knew a crusty, ill-tempered old woman, who lived alone in one very dismal room, with no apparent means of support but her parish allowance and occasional charity. Her neighbours resented her caustic tongue, so her solitude was seldom invaded, but at vague intervals she started on a pilgrimage among old acquaintances, from each of whom she exacted a contribution of at least one penny, and on the proceeds of the tour she got satisfactorily drunk. The deliberation of what she did gave it an ugly look, and she was appealed to and denounced as peculiarly a sinner, but only once,

as I was told, did she retort — " Wad ye grudge me my
one chance o' getting clean out o' ' the Pans,' wi' a sup of
whisky? " You see in that sombre, embittered nature
there remained this thin streak of poetry, the craving for
an imaginative escape from the dreariness of her days, so
the pious preachings addressed to a supposed moral degradation did not touch her where she really lived. We, men
and women, are queer creatures, dust of the earth and
breath of God, and (if effectively we are to help a neighbour forward we must get so close to him as to understand
him.) Even of our Lord Jesus it is written (v. 17) that He
could only become a merciful and faithful High Priest
(actually fit for His chosen task) by being made like unto
His brethren; and if we are to share in His work the same
demand is unescapable for us.

It is never easy to make any substantial change in the
character and habits of others. Most of the people in our
churches are living in the main as they always have lived,
and as their fathers lived before them — douce, decent,
church-going folk. In an Anglican Church they would
unite with others in calling themselves " miserable offenders," but they would not strictly mean it, for they
are not really miserable, and inwardly they do not reckon
themselves as terribly in offence; so what chance is there
of making them, in their self-complacency, realize that
they are missing something high and covetable which, at
any moment, might be theirs? Even in a case very imper-
fectly parallel we can recognize this necessity of getting
close to one another: if a musician, sensitive in every fibre,
were constrained for his livelihood to teach a child with
little music in her, his prospect of success would in any

case be poor, but if he simply denounced his shivering victim as fool and blockhead he would have no chance at all. So far as he can he must come to the child's level, practising friendliness and infinite patience, and welcoming even the feeblest indication of awakening interest. Thus he might make progress, but not otherwise. Or take an insensibility of another kind: some people are always in debt and are never a whit troubled about what their creditors may suffer. I remember a man of this sort sternly reproving his distracted wife (who had to face the tradesmen) for using a money present which she had got in paying one particularly urgent bill, since, in his view, this was a wanton flinging away of what would have kept him in pocket-money for a fortnight. " Why on earth did you pay that? " he asked; " are there not plenty other things to pay? " Now is there any way of awakening conscience in such a creature? Wesley in his Journal tells of a plan which did succeed, although far oftener it might have failed. Two of his lay preachers became close friends, and the one, discovering that the other was careless about money and deep in debt, reminded him that Christians must first of all be just, and added as an obvious plan, — " We'll put our pays together and live hard, and what we save will pay the debt." We might not be prepared for so unreserved a fellowship in effort and self-denial, but it certainly was the method which Jesus followed in procuring our salvation. Sanctifier and sanctified must be of one group, says our author: it was thus that deliverance was brought to men, and thus it still must come. To raise us from our ghastly, dead life of contentment with meaner things, He became a real man, tempted as we are, and like us learning by the things which He suffered. Lest the reality of Christ's temptation should be underrated, our author (Ch. 5:7) points to Gethsemane, with its strong crying and tears, and to Calvary and His endurance of death (Ch. 2:9), and he declares that it was only through His sharing in such experience that Jesus was made fit for His office of High Priest and Pioneer of Salvation: apart from this His work would have remained undone. And what was true of Him is certainly not less true of us in our ministry: if effectively we are to help our fellows we must get close to them. It used to be told of a very prominent Scottish minister that, in his parish rounds, he called upon a radical cobbler, prickly as any porcupine, who greeted him with the question, " Do you come here as a minister or as a friend? " To which the poor, vain creature replied, " I do not visit cobblers as friends." " He who sanctifieth and they who are sanctified must be of one group," so that the just requisite of a right ministry is that the minister should himself be as a man with men.

2. A second characteristic of our Lord's ministry on which special stress is laid, though it lies close to the first, is that of active sympathy with our human infirmities (Ch. 4:15), and though defect at this point might seem to be peculiarly the temptation of the stern Puritans, it is lamentably common elsewhere. One bewildering example of such failure is furnished by John Wesley in the code of rules which he drafted for his school at Kingswood near Bristol. He was forty-five years old and ought to have had sense, yet he laid it down that no games were to be allowed in the school or the grounds, and he sagely adds that " he who plays when he is a child will play when

he is a man." No holidays were given, and a child, once admitted to the school, stayed there until he left for good. The household, old and young, had to rise at four in the morning, and spend the first hour in private reading and meditation, in prayer and singing, and on Friday they all fasted until three in the afternoon. Such nature-defying foolishness ought at once to have been recognized as such and corrected; but after thirty-five years (in 1783) Wesley still records in his Journal: " The children ought never to play, but they do every day, and even in the school. They run about in the wood, and mix and even fight with the colliers' children. . . . They are not religious: they have not the power and hardly the form of it." One is glad to read of the bairns as running about in the wood and fighting with the little colliers: it is a welcome touch of wholesome nature. But think of a man engaged in the task of leading his fellows to reality and to God, and yet understanding them so badly!

In contrast with such incredible blundering the true High Priest is described as able to make allowance for the ignorant and the erring. An interesting word (not found again in Scripture and never in the Classics) is used which means to feel moderately, to keep a mid course between explosions of anger and a lazy indulgence. This, certainly, was a master gift in Jesus, who could understand *why* men go wrong, and thus could help them in their straying. And if we are to share in His task we must cultivate the same mind, lest by a stupid pedantry we should give rise to reaction and revolt, not against ourselves only but against the Church and the Christian name.

3. A third qualification for His office which Jesus pos-

sessed was His freedom from anything of the official: His priesthood was not conferred upon Him from without but was rooted in Himself. The Latin saying is familiar that " the cowl does not make the monk "; and unless a man have something in him of the priestly nature, no Church and no external form can ever constitute him an open channel of God's grace to men. It is true that in some communions and in most of the pagan cults the character of the priest is secondary: he may even be a notorious loose-liver, but his official standing secures that his sacraments and his absolution remain valid. In a brief life of Liddon, George Russell describes his hero as halting in a portrait gallery before the representation of a peculiarly animal and bloated figure — a bishop — and exclaiming, " How strange that, in the Providence of God, grace should have had to be transmitted to Mr. Keble through that person! " Liddon called it strange, our author would have dismissed it as impossible, for, in his eyes, such a person could not transmit grace; being the man he was he could only obstruct it.

In our Epistle this point is treated as fundamental. The author's pattern of priesthood is Melchizedek, who, in the mists of early history, stands out alone " without father, without mother, without descent " (Ch. 7:3), following in no orthodox succession, but having his sole title in himself. And in this Jesus is like to him. " If He were still on earth," it is admitted (Ch. 8:4), " He would not be a priest at all ": " He belonged to a tribe of which no man gave attendance at the altar " (Ch. 7:13), and He was not consecrated according to any accepted rules. Technical qualifications He thus had none, but then how overwhelming were His personal qualifications! The same contrast appears in connection with every noble task. Even a king, whose title at law is unassailable, who can dress the part to perfection and is master of all the etiquette of his position, if he has nothing in himself to govern by, must remain a pitifully, and sometimes a disastrously, helpless figure on his throne. Napoleon at St. Helena once confessed that, in company with the Czar and the King of Prussia, he had sometimes wondered if he knew anything about soldiering, for their detailed knowledge as to the proper length of a tunic or the number of buttons on a sleeve so far outreached his own. Aye, but when he faced their armies in the field, which of them had the knowledge that mattered? And this is supremely true of the ministry: unless a man have a heart for the business — a nature towards his people and a nature towards God — he is essentially an encumbrance, even if his church be crowded to the doors. A wise man, in whom these personal qualities are present, will welcome the recognition of the Church as giving support; but if these are lacking, the most correct and venerable forms of institution will leave him as they found him — an outsider and intruder. That is our author's emphatic teaching: a priest, who is to help men aright, must be such by nature, as Jesus was, and not as an official.

4. The last of the qualifications for this priesthood which I need mention, is that the man must be, as Jesus was, at home with God. It is his business to declare God's mind towards men and to awaken in them a desire after Him, which cannot be achieved unless the priest has seen the Father and known His mind. Of prophets who failed

through lack of this furnishing, Jeremiah declares (Jer. 23:22), " If they had stood in my council they would have turned my people from their evil ways," and of those priests, estranged from God, who yet dared in His name to bless the people, it is savagely announced (Mal. 2:3), "I will rebuke your arm upraised in blessing: I will spread dung upon your face, even the dung of your temple feasts, and ye shall be carted away with it."

But no such challenge could touch our High Priest, since He Himself belonged to the shrine. " Such was the High Priest for us," it is said (Heb. 7:26), " holy, inno-cent, unstained, lifted high above the heavens, who needs not like others to offer sacrifices first for sins of His own "; and, striking still higher, our author says again, " To which even of the angels did God ever say — Thou are my Son? " John is not content to declare of his Lord (John 1:1), " In the beginning He was with God "; he later adds the illuminating word (Ch. 13), " No man has ascended into heaven but He who came down from heaven, even the Son of man *who is in heaven*." It is true that the words in italics do not appear in some of the best manuscripts, and thus they may not be John's own, but the authority for them carries us back into the second century, so that at least they record a very early impression of what Jesus was like. Whilst He lived in Galilee, labouring at a trade and fulfilling the duties of a home, He already to His deeper seeing neighbours seemed to carry about with Him an air of mysterious elevation, like one whose essential citizenship was in heaven. Thus standing in God's coun-cil and speaking the words which God supplied, He was and He is able to turn men from evil ways.

In rough outline I have shown you what our author teaches about our need of a priest and the kind of priest we need. Nature itself seems to keep us low in a world of poor and perishing things, and this bias of nature is exaggerated by the self-indulgence which so clogs our nobler part as to hold us back from the higher world of realities, so our need of a Priest-Forerunner is absolute. He must be one of ourselves and able thus to understand and sympathize; He must not be an official but a person with a heart for the tasks assigned; and most of all, He must be one living with God and in God, if He is to be able to bring us to God. In this there is much which might scare us, and yet He has left us an example that we should follow in His steps. We hold a richer doctrine of Christ's nature than Matthew Arnold ever attained, and yet, if we are wise, we may say with him:

> " Was Christ a man like us? Oh, let us see
> If we then too can be such men as He! "

Certainly if in our ministry we would have lasting success we must steadily keep before us the pattern of His ministry as our guide and rule.

THE MAKING OF A PREACHER —
THROUGH KNOWLEDGE OF GOD

YESTERDAY we considered a New Testament Platonist's view of the priest's task in such a world as this and some qualities of character which enabled Jesus to fulfil that task. I noted that these qualities are not exclusively to be found in Jesus but may at least be sought for and cultivated by us, so to-day and to-morrow I propose to talk of things indispensable in the making of a preacher.

Some students appear scarcely to realize that, except in external matters like elocution, any such making is required. They have been born loquacious, so for them the preacher's business, on the side of public speaking, has no terrors. " A blind man can ay talk," as our fathers used to say. An interesting pamphlet of Charles II's days discusses the causes which had brought contempt on religion and the clergy, and stress is laid on " the knack of preaching " as one of the chief of these. This knack made preaching so easy that, as the writer says, " unless a man be excessively dull he can, without warning, lay hold of any text in Scripture, and tear and tumble it until the hour-glass runs out." This company of glib talkers is with us still, for ignorance of a subject has seldom blocked the way to the most copious discoursing upon it. When George Adam Smith was in the splendour of his Aberdeen ministry a neighbour exhorted him to master shorthand, since thus he would be able to write six or even ten sermons in a week instead of two: to which he had modestly to reply that his slow longhand could generally keep pace with the flow of his essential ideas. What a preacher most requires is not the cultivation of fluency and professional dexterities of the surface, but qualities of character, the gift of inward understanding, and, in particular, a personal knowledge of God.

In describing Wesley's mastery over hostile mobs, Quiller-Couch remarks: " For aught that I can discern he had no great eloquence and said little that his hearers might not have heard on any Sunday in their own churches: his voice was hoarse from overwork and his manner was not winning, yet notorious ruffians were seen sobbing like children, and some were writhing on the ground like the demoniacs in the Gospels. . . . One secret of his power was that he always spoke with authority, and another was his kingly neglect of trifles, for he paid no heed to the signs which made his hearers judge of themselves and others as lost beyond recovery." The secrets of his success on its human side were thus in his character and not in any external attraction. When Bunyan at the Interpreter's house depicts his ideal minister, it is as one who had " the law of truth upon his lips, the world behind his back, and who stood as if he pleaded with men . . ." This, says Bunyan, is " the only man whom the Lord of the place whither thou art going hath authorized to be thy guide." " *The only man authorized to be thy guide*," for to Bunyan it was clear that no ministry can be valid which does not rest upon such qualifications as unworldliness and an eager desire for the salvation of men. John Owen, the Puritan, tells in one of his sermons of an unfortunate who had on his hands a dead body which, for the moment, he wished to pass as living, so he propped it on a seat, but it fell, and when with greater care he tried again, it fell again; whereupon he ruefully muttered, " *Oportet esse aliquid intus* — it needs something inside it." Now this *aliquid intus* is the main secret of a right ministry, and where it is absent no outward appearance of success can redeem it from essential failure. In one of his novels George Macdonald depicts a triumphantly popular preacher in Aberdeen, who drew great audiences and also wrote sentimental hymns, and thus " exercised a double influence for the humiliation of Christianity." The man was so obtrusively hollow — ambitious and self-seeking — that serious observers outside the Church were, by the very greatness of his success, convinced that the Church of Christ has a vicious taste for shams. " He who enters not in by the door," said Jesus, " but climbeth up some other way, the same is a thief and a robber."

It is interesting to note how persistently Milton presses a like demand on all would-be poets. The poet's soul, he asserts, ought to contain " the perfect shape of what is wise and just and good," and to keep this unspoiled he must in himself maintain " a pure mind in a pure body." " He who would not be frustrated in his hope hereafter to write well of laudable things ought himself to be a true poem — that is, a composition and pattern of the best and honourablest things, not presuming to write high praises of heroic men or famous cities unless in himself he have the experience and the practice of all that is praiseworthy." Heights like these are not to be attained without God, so Milton bids the poet " pray devoutly to that Eternal Spirit who alone can enrich with knowledge and utterance, sending out His seraphim with hallowed fire to touch and purify the lips of whom He pleases." Thus, as you see, to Milton it was clear that without this gift of " something within " no greater work need be attempted. Certainly this rule applies to your intended calling. Milton speaks of " singing high praises of heroic men and famous cities," but do you consider it an easier task to proclaim " the Gospel of the glory of the blessed God "? If the poet's soul must contain " the perfect shape of the good and the wise and the just " can this be less essential for a preacher? I have had students quite decently equipped upon the surface, correct in their behaviour, with good appearance and address, and with such sufficiency of book-learning as set them above any fear of examiners. The one gap in their furnishing was that they had no piety — no living interest in God and His purposes and no active concern for the distresses of their fellows. In Dante's terrible words they were " neither for God nor for God's enemies, but for themselves." They easily mastered the communicable tricks of the trade, and some of them have enjoyed considerable success, but the vital preparation was lacking. " Be a good man, my dear," said Scott when he was dying; " be religious, be a good man! " This must always be considered first.

There are two ways in which such inward piety may help a man in his preaching: on the one hand, his transparent sincerity lends force to everything he says, and makes him a living epistle of Christ. Sir Philip Sidney was

not only a gallant soldier and a darling of Elizabeth's
Court, a close friend reports that in him there was visible

> " A sweet, attractive kind of grace,
>   A full assurance borne by looks,
> Continual comfort in a face,
>   The lineaments of Gospel books."

Such a character must have spoken more loudly than any
words. Augustine wrote (quoted by John Ker), " In order
to his being obediently listened to, the life of the teacher
is of greater weight than any splendour of diction "
(*granditas dictionis*). When Dr. Wilson of the Barclay
Church in Edinburgh died, Principal Rainy spoke of the
value for their whole community of having within it a
man whom you could not see on the street without wondering on what unselfish errand he was hastening. Paul's
passionate desire for his Galatian friends (Gal. 4:19) was
that " Christ might be formed in them," actually taking
shape and becoming visible in them, and though this may
seem beyond us yet, we surely at least may endeavour
after it. At the Free Church Assembly of 1844, amid the
enthusiasm of triumphant beginnings, a preacher pled
with his brethren that they should never enter a pulpit
without something of Christ's temper when He wept over
the city: the inner and the outer, the emotion and the utterance, must be in harmony, if any preaching is to de-
serve a hearing. " Though I speak with the tongues of
men and of angels," says Paul (that is, with dazzling eloquence and even with an air of heavenly inspiration), " if
I have not love I am nothing but a noisy gong." In seeking ordination your professed desire is to help your fellows

in their tangled task of living by exhibiting Jesus Christ to them and enlisting them for His service; but if you yourself are self-indulgent and conceited and worldly the contrast between you and Him is grotesque and even shocking, and if you fail the reason will be in yourself.

The other way in which his inward piety gives force to a man's preaching is less obtrusive but scarcely less important. How can anyone with effect speak of things which he does not know? In particular, how can he proclaim deliverance and a new life with any energy of conviction if he has had no experience of these? Paul tells us that his own pertinacity in labour was based upon his experience: " Inasmuch as I have received mercy I do not lose heart " (II Cor. 4:1). His memory of the road by which he had travelled and of the grace which had transformed his own life gave confidence and effect to his words; but, on the other hand, nothing has been so injurious to the Church's good name as the ministry of men who have offered themselves as guides, knowing nothing of the way. Such persons are not a new plague: already in the second century Hermas speaks of those who " empty themselves, give empty answers to empty people," and Milton denounces those in his day who posed as preachers though they had nothing to give, so " the hungry sheep look up and are not fed." What knowledge of the Divine such men possess is not, in any true sense, their own but has been taken over by them from others. In passing through so many hands its freshness is bound to have faded, but even though it be shop soiled they are confident that it still can find a market. " Their fear of me is a tradition of men which has been taught them," is

Isaiah's scornful description (Isa. 29:13) of this numerous class. Their words may be good enough, but the preacher has no personal title to them, for he does not of himself know that they are true. Of Seneca, the moralist, who, at the same time, managed to be a favourite of Nero's, Emerson sternly declares, " His thoughts are excellent, if only he had the right to utter them." Gentlemen, you must see to it that no such appalling condemnation shall be deserved by you.

Jeremiah wittily describes all preachers of this sort (Jer. 23:31): " They use their tongues and say — Thus saith the Lord ": their *tongues*, you see, for no deeper faculty in them is engaged; their preaching proceeds from the loquacious levels of their nature. And again, more fiercely, he says, " They steal my words, every man from his neighbour, and say — Thus saith the Lord " (v. 30). Since they have nothing of their own they have to make out an existence as sorners and mendicants, depending on whatever scraps may come their way. A picturesque scrap of student slang, which most unfittingly was flung at Paul by the Athenians, fits these men like a glove: in our version it appears as " this babbler," which is pointless, for the word means a picker up of seeds like a bird on a harvest field. Later it was used of loafers in a market who pounced on any fallen apple or onion for a meal; and finally, with the shrewd malice of students, it was applied to would-be teachers, who made a display with what they had filched from others. " They steal my words ": do not let yourselves sink to that degradation!

In thus insisting that a preacher should have thoughts which are his own, I in no way mean that his thoughts should all be novel. Paul repeatedly refers to " my gospel " or " our gospel," but if you examine the passages you will find nothing distinctively Pauline in them. They are concerned with central Christian commonplaces like the Resurrection of Jesus (II Tim. 2:8), the call to salvation and eternal glory (II Thess. 2:14), the certainty that Jesus is to be the Judge of men (Rom. 2:16). These were not peculiarities or originalities of Paul's, but they had captured his mind and set his heart on fire, so that they had become his convictions, parts of his gospel, always to be proclaimed by him as with his signature attached. This experience of being freshly captured by an idea is met with on every level of intelligence: I remember a simple lass in Fife who came with shining face one Easter Sunday to tell her minister that on that day she had discovered that Jesus was actually alive. Of course, from her childhood she had known that this was asserted, and she had never doubted it, but never before had she felt the gladness and the liberation which the Resurrection can secure; so to her it had only now become a power of life and her very own. At the other extreme may be set Coleridge's familiar claim that in the Bible there is more which had *found* him, and found him at greater depths of his being, than in all other books put together. Truths set down in Scripture as for everyone had struck home to him, Coleridge, at the very roots of his nature, and had compelled in him a personal assent. A man who starts upon his ministry with even a few truths thus attested to his heart may have nothing to say which has not often before been uttered, but his message is invested with a freshness of feeling and delight, because to him it is no carried story but a discovery. Paul's delightful description of the experience (Eph. 1:18) is, " The eyes of your *heart* being enlightened so that ye know ": of your *heart*, not of your *understanding*, as in our version, for what Paul had in mind was not some gain in intellectual apprehension but a fresh feeling in presence of things which might have been long familiar, and yet could change for any man the whole colour of existence. Now preaching, as Phillips Brooks has said, is " truth through personality," truth vitalized by personal experience, and whenever it loses this quality, it may be clever and eloquent, but, as Paul would have said, it is like a tinkling cymbal, musical but rather futile.

When a truth has thus found a man there may be much for him to do in the way of deepening and securing his hold upon it, just as of Scripture we are admonished to " read, mark, learn, and inwardly digest " it. Digestion, after all, is just a familiar kind of appropriation, through which what was foreign passes into our substance and becomes a fresh spring of our energies. In his whimsical way Samuel Butler insists that eating is always a kind of proselytizing: " We convert the food, or try to convert it, to our way of thinking, and if it sticks to its opinion and declines to be converted we say that it disagrees with us," and the jest has obvious applications in the region through which we are travelling. A truth discovered should not be left simply as it has come to us; it should be explored and applied, and thus it is confirmed. The prophets repeatedly employ the same homely image of eating: " Thy word was found and I did eat it, and it was to me the joy and rejoicing of my heart," says Jeremiah (Jer. 15:16). Ezekiel (Ezek. 2:8 to 3:3 and Rev. 10:8–10) elaborates the image a little, but his main point is plain: " He said to me, Son of man, eat this scroll, and then go and speak to the house of Israel." It would seem that before a message can effectively be transmitted it must first be digested by the preacher himself and become part of his own life. If this condition be ignored and the Gospel uttered in an impersonal way failure can scarcely be avoided. Listen to Newman's confession about his own work at one period: " I look on myself very much as a piece of glass, which transmits heat but remains cold itself. . . . I have a vivid perception of the consequences of certain principles, a considerable intellectual capacity of drawing them out, and a rhetorical or histrionic power of representing them; but I believe myself at heart to be nearly hollow, with little love and little self-denial." It may be that the confession was the morbid utterance of a passing mood, but it is the kind of judgment from which a sincere man must shrink in dismay. It asserts the possibility of becoming a master in our business and yet making nothing of it, for Newman's closing words — " with little love and little self-denial " — irresistibly remind us of the Apostle's warning — " though I speak with the tongues of men and of angels but have not love, I am like a noisy gong." The Bible order in preaching is unmistakable — " I believe and therefore do I speak " (Ps. 116:10; II Cor. 4:13): the faith, however fragmentary, has to come first, and there is no preparation for a preacher like him who can say, " It pleased God to reveal His Son in me."

But if personal experience is thus made central is it not bound to narrow the range of topics in our preaching and make our work monotonous? Each of us may feel that what he has thus discovered is the fruit of only one man's experience, with all the gaps and omissions and blind spots which are inevitable, and that, for this reason, much which it would be good for people to hear may be overlooked. I doubt if that is a fatal defect in preaching if such narrowing of range leads to more of concentration; as Hesiod said twenty-five hundred years ago, " The half is better than the whole." That great German evangelist, Hofacker, deplored the fact that " in the pulpit we have so many words which never touch on Him," for preaching which left Christ out to him seemed preaching spoiled. A wise man will always be guided in his choice of topics by consideration for what his people most need and for what they are able to understand, but he will also give heed to his own limitations. At Athens, as Luke tells us, Paul sought to meet the philosophers on their own ground, but even he made little of it, so when he passed on to Corinth he determined (I Cor. 2:2) " to know nothing among them save Jesus Christ and Him as the Crucified." That was a deliberate narrowing of range with a view to effect, and as the generations pass, the angle of approach to men may have to be modified for the same reason. There was a time when the terrors of Hell had a central place in orthodox sermons, so that with little exaggeration Burns could describe a preacher as mounting the pulpit " wi' tidings o' damnation." But the balance of feeling and experience has been altered, and in justice to the effect of our message we must lay the emphasis at a different point. A supreme theologian and preacher like Schleiermacher found himself constrained

to treat the so-called " doctrines of the Last Things " as
of far less definiteness and certainty than other assertions
of faith, which can be tested and confirmed by human
experience. Inevitably our thoughts of all that concerns
the Last Judgment and the conditions of doom or blessed-
ness in the future life must be coloured by speculation
and surmise: inference and desire have more to do with
them than explicit revelation. So Schleiermacher deals
with them in a separate section as of less authority and
importance: they are *prophetische Lehrstücke* — pro-
phetic fragments of teaching, anticipations rather than
declarations.

On this point of deliberately narrowing our range of
topics Luther's witness and example are supremely instructive. In his day there was much debate about Predes-
tination and its icy altitudes, and he bluntly cautions his
preachers to begin always near the ground where, with
Christ, they could always find the Father: if you are ambitious, he said, and begin at the top, you will likely tumble and break your necks. " We preachers are like babies,
only learning to speak, who can as yet utter nothing but
half words and quarter words "; so any consideration by a
preacher of his own capacity would keep him in the region of simple and central things. And, in view of the people's capacity, Luther's advice is not less homely: " I do
not aim very high in my pulpit at Wittenberg, as if I were
addressing none but scholars and doctors and magistrates,
of whom there may be forty in the building, for there are
also present two thousand plain folk and lads and lasses,
and to them I speak as their need requires. If the others
do not like it, the door is open, and they are free to de-

part." History assures us that they did not depart, for though he talked thus simply, learned and unlearned alike crowded about him whenever he preached, just as people gather in about a fire on a wintry night. Preachers have seldom suffered by holding to what is elementary in the Gospel; and it is a poor account of anyone who confesses that he cannot keep interest alive in the love-revealing, love-inspiring truths which are the treasure of the simple.

I suppose there always will be men who love to splurge and talk ambitiously of anything and everything, but this desire of theirs to rove is mainly due to their failure to explore the great central things, which are revealed to the childlike. For that revelation is never at an end. When Paul bids Timothy defend the Gospel as a trust committed to his care, he adds one instructive note (II Tim. 1:14): "That splendid trust you must always guard through the Holy Spirit who dwelleth in us." That is to say — the Gospel can only successfully be defended as it is continually rediscovered, through the working of that Spirit who takes of the things of Christ and shows them unto us. Thus we come back to the lesson of John Owen's grim illustration and read as the fundamental rule for every preacher, " *Oportet esse aliquid intus* — it needs something inside it," for he who lacks this is nothing worth.

THE MAKING OF A PREACHER —
THROUGH THE KNOWLEDGE OF MAN

In addition to this knowledge of God of which I have spoken, it is indispensable for a preacher that he should know men, what they are and how they think and feel. It is a teacher's maxim that if with success you are to teach Tommy Latin you must not only know some Latin you must know Tommy; and on a higher level we read (Heb. 5:1, 2) that " every High Priest taken from among men must be able to make allowance for the ignorant and the erring," for without such knowledge of his clients his peculiar work cannot be done. Of all our attempts to judge our fellow ill-doers Burns has said,

> " One thing must still be greatly dark —
> The moving why they do it."

And yet for the discharging of our task we must, at least in some degree, penetrate the mystery.

And here we run at once upon a common obstacle, for many candidates for the ministry are little concerned deeply to know their people. In youthful self-importance a lad is tempted to think first of the people as somehow there for *him*, like an organ to be practised on, or the first step of a ladder on which he may climb to eminence. Forty years ago I used to know pretty well a men's club in

Edinburgh to which students from the New College used to go down to give help: but some offence had been given, and one of the members slyly said to me, " We ken fine that thae lads are wanting to learn aff us, and we're no going to let them learn much." No doubt, my friend was greatly less than just to the students, but unfortunately it is true that through shyness or self-engrossment or conceit many lads come up with no hearty, human interest in their neighbours. Renan tells against himself how, when he was studying for the priesthood, a professor came on him one day sitting in the College park, wrapped in a thick greatcoat, and very much at his ease over an engrossing book. The professor exclaimed: " Ah, the wee darling, how cosy he looks there! For any sake, do nothing to disturb him! And that is what he will be like all his days. And when the care of souls comes upon him, he will still be lost in his books, and when he is called to a duty he will exclaim, ' Why cannot you leave me in peace? ' " The shot went home, as Renan admits: " I was distressed by it, but I was not converted." And many who have none of Renan's excuse of passionate studiousness exhibit the same temper of detachment, which handicaps them in all their ministry. They sit apart, indifferent to the deeper needs of their fellows, and thus they cannot possibly devise a remedy.

It is never easy to come quite close to our neighbours, soul with soul. Keble speaks of " our hermit spirits," for there is an element of loneliness in each of us: " The heart knows its own bitterness, and a stranger intermeddleth not with its joy." But there are gifts or faculties of nature by which the chasms dividing us may be crossed, and we may enter, at least in some degree, into the joy and grief, the temptation and bewilderment, of the people about us. Chief among these gifts are love and imagination and, in a less degree, humour, and a host of the failures and disasters in the ministry are due to lack of these. Shelley asserts that " the great secret of morals is love, since it takes us out of our own nature and leads us to identify ourselves with others "; and he goes on, " If a man is to be greatly good [and surely as ministers we ought to share in this ambition] he must imagine intensely and comprehensively, so that the pains and pleasures of others come home to him as his own." But if love and imagination be accepted why should humour be dragged in? Is it anything more than an amiable fondness for a joke? In his brilliant study of Dickens, George Gissing declares that " humour is inseparable from charity: it not only enabled Dickens to see some coarse creature as an amusing person, it inspired him with that large tolerance which looks through things external, gives its full weight to circumstance, and preserves modesty and humility in our human judgments." It may be broadly said that sympathy is essential to complete humour, which is a vastly richer gift than wit, sparkling and sometimes wounding. Humour is that kindly irradiation of nature which helps us to recognize our kinships and thus to make allowance for others, and it helps us, which is very important, on occasion to laugh at ourselves. Aye, humour is a vital gift, and a wholly humourless minister is a desolating object. Now these three gifts have all a place of right in our human constitution, and anyone born without them would seem to be only half a man, whereas the hope which Paul holds out before us (Eph. 4:13) is that of " attaining to a full-grown man." And this is my main subject — the making of a man worthy to be called " a *fit* minister of the New Covenant " (II Cor. 3:6). We may feel that of a man without humour and without human kindness nothing can ever be made, but I cling to the belief that something may be achieved even by drawing attention to the defect. Renan allows that though he was not converted by his master's irony, he was distressed by it, which might have been the beginning of better things; so I propose now to exhibit to you on some of its many sides this narrowness of nature, outside of the needs and griefs and hopes of others, that you may see how variously it may interfere with the work we have to do.

One obvious consequence of it is the entire irrelevance of many sermons to the thoughts and needs of the people addressed: the preacher imagines that he can make something of a text, but he never considers whether that something will be of any use to the long-suffering people. More than forty years ago a young friend of mine went out as an engineer to the construction works on the Great Dam on the Upper Nile. His post was extremely isolated, and for months together in the hot season he and his comrades never saw a parson, and in their time of leisure they were left exposed to the fierce temptations of vacancy and of evil example. On one occasion a chaplain did arrive to take a service, and as an appropriate subject of address to these exiled lads he chose the duty of observing all the Saints' Days in the calendar, as if they had been a group of the devout widows and spinsters in his home congregation. In his next letter home my friend denounced the idiocy of such a parson and the folly of a Church which had sent him. Clearly he was a first-prize idiot, and he may have been beyond correction, for " though thou bray a fool in the mortar, yet will not his folly depart from him " (Prov. 27:22). But you must not think of him as a unique exception. The criminal stupidity of his choice of topic was due to what is deplorably common in all Churches — the failure to think of the audience and its needs. How often at a Service of Preparation for Communion have I heard a man making display of his own gifts by delivering his most brilliant recent discourse, hard, clever, undevout, whilst " the hungry sheep looked up, and were not fed."

One of the most ludicrous examples of this pulpit detachment from the life and feeling of the people is found in Augustine's *Confessions*. He relates how once, with a pack of riotous companions, he raided an orchard and stripped a pear tree, and then, without any regard for due proportion, he lets his homiletic thunders loose: " I resolved to steal and I did steal, not from any pressure of want or penury, but from the scorn of justice and the full-fed insolence of sin. The pears were not tempting either to the eye or the taste, and of the load we carried away we only ate a few, and threw the rest to the pigs. . . . A ruined soul was I, breaking from Thy starry heavens into outer darkness, and seeking no other reward from shame than the shame itself." A little later it occurs to him that the daftness of a group had something to do with the prank, and he asks " Was there not something besides the theft which attracted me? Nay, nothing else, for even that something was nothing." All the infectious joys of companionship he dismisses in one coarse phrase: " I need not have increased the itching of my lust by rubbing like a hog against my mates." The whole long passage is the idlest of stage thunder, and it reveals nothing but the great man's inability to enter into the feelings of a mischievous boy; which suggests a grievous defect in his manhood. An old Scotswoman, in talking of the boyhood of Professor Bruce, showed herself a wiser psychologist than Augustine when she said, " He was a wild laddie, but he wasna deevilish." Gentlemen, without some gift of sympathetic imagination our preaching may go wildly astray, even if we were as eloquent as Augustine.

The other day I detailed to you some of the preposterous regulations devised by Wesley for his school at Kingswood. Now you must not suppose that these were due to some vicious hardness of nature or to anything worse than lack of imagination, for the man practised even more than he prescribed. We never read of his enjoying a game or feeling the want of one; he attributed his unbroken health on to extreme age to his habit of preaching at five or six in the morning, whenever he had the chance; and he magnified the spiritual value of fasting. Thus everything which he exacted from the children would to him appear easy and even profitable. Yet surely a grown man ought to have realized that a school is seldom filled with John Wesleys, and that what suited him might come on the scholars as sheer martyrdom and mutilation. The trouble was that he had not learned to think and feel outside of himself, so that when he was eighty he was still perplexed and saddened because of the deplorable propensity of children to play games even in his school.

It is imagination, as Shelley says, which " brings the

pains and pleasures home to us as our own," and in a ludicrous but lamentably common example we may see what the want of it in a minister may do. A prominent churchman had died, and a garrulous friend was asked to take the Committal Prayer in the cemetery. A large company gathered, but unfortunately, when the coffin was about to be lowered, the heavens opened and a terrific deluge came down. The drumming of rain on umbrellas made every other sound inaudible, but the officiating minister felt that he must do himself and the occasion justice, and for almost fifteen minutes he held on his way, regardless of the growing misery of the company. His jaws could be seen to open and shut, but no articulate word came through, and a cynical old minister muttered to his neighbour, " Do you think he kens it's raining? " That impatient crowd was made a victim to the self-importance and the lack of imagination of a minister. This may seem trivial, but it is not merely trivial: on a very similar occasion some months ago a big farmer in leaving the kirkyard exclaimed vehemently against the offending parson, " That is the kind of man who drives us out of the kirk."

Or take as another instance the case of a decent Free Church minister, forty or fifty years ago, who honestly did his work in a hard, unimaginative fashion, neglecting none of his duties, and sparing no pains in producing his elaborately rhetorical sermons. His visitation was ruled by a too rigorous time-table which never allowed more than so many minutes to any household. If, through any accident, time were lost early in his round the later visits must be curtailed in order that his full task for the day might be completed, and he get home in good time for his dinner. One evening, on entering the home of a very poor and very solitary woman, he looked at his watch and said, " I see I can only give you seven minutes ": " Aweel, if that is a' ye needna sit down." You see, he was an official and not a full-grown man: he was thinking more of his carefully ordered plans and his punctual meals than of the woman in her chilling loneliness or of troubles which she might have been storing up for him when he came; so he left her wounded and insulted, and she never forgot. And it was lack of imagination which poisoned everything.

The same lack of sympathetic imagination gives colour also to a man's thinking, and thus to his preaching. First of all, as we have seen, it makes his sermons irrelevant to the actual situations, and, it may be, to any human situation. Dr. Robertson Nicoll once headed an article on two theological books with the significant title " Two Angelic Doctors," for to him the books seemed to have been written by friendly outsiders and not by men in the fierce thick of things, who could know what their fellows are and what they need. Fifty years ago we had a minister, a courteous gentleman of scholarly interests, of whom his friend Henry Drummond once said to me, " He is a juiceless creature: you can bear even with an ass if he has juice, but he has no juice." I knew him too slightly to feel the aptness of the description, but soon after I heard him read a paper in a club which helped me to understand. His subject was the Incarnation, a theme which touches life at every point, but to the writer the question calling for exploration was the difference made in Heaven when the Word was made flesh. Earth then was made richer, but, by the rules of plain arithmetic, Heaven must surely have become by so much emptier: the earthly plus must have been balanced by a heavenly minus. In what, then, did this minus consist? Of the power and the passion of this Divine event, into which angels desire to look, he had little to say: the discussion throughout was aridly speculative and even spectral. He was not concerned with questions in which life is at stake, but, in true scholastic fashion, he was chasing his own tail like a dog just for exercise and amusement. I never heard him preach, but I cannot imagine that he preached humanly, for he was a juiceless creature; and there are multitudes of his class, without his scholarship, unable to get outside of themselves, and to think and feel along with their fellows.

But now, since the gain is so great for him who possesses love and imagination and humour, can nothing be done for the many decent creatures who are poor in these? " Can the Ethiopian change his skin or the leopard his spots? " Is there any way for a man to become " a fit minister " who is self-engrossed and shrinks from any contact, like a snail into its shell? Or must he always remain a blundering outsider, such as I have described? There can be no doubt that such a man is terribly handicapped, but is it not possible for these gifts to be cultivated? If it is taken by itself, the parable of the Sower is a very depressing Scripture, since it suggests that, if a man's nature is shallow or if it is foul with weeds, he will make no enduring good of the Gospel message. But even the best of images fails at some point, and the parable has not room within it for the processes by which the shallow ground may be deepened, and the preoccupied heart made able to receive the word of life. A man's birth is not of necessity his doom, and people, by nature unimaginative and even selfish, may acquire the habit of looking and living outside the narrow circle of their own interests. In his *Wilhelm Meister* Goethe lays it down that reverence is not native in men, it has to be acquired; and in the province through which Meister travelled he found all the boys engaged in securing this preparation for a complete life. They were tutored first in reverence for things and powers above them, to look up and adore; then in reverence for those on their own level, to honour all men and love the brethren; and thus they came to their hardest lesson, to the learning of reverence for what might seem beneath them — the ignorant and the overlooked, the weak creatures and the broken lives. So elaborate a training may seem impossible, but the vital idea of the scheme should never be forgotten — that human nature can be enriched and that qualities of character may be acquired. Frederick Robertson somewhere says that " courtesy of manner often begets courtesy of heart," by which, I suppose, he meant that the merely social drill, which constrains us, even at a meal, to consider other people first, may work inwardly until, through habit, it creates something like an instinct of courtesy. Progress certainly can be made, but not without deliberate effort and self-schooling. In Shelley's words, " Love is that which carries us out from the narrowness of our own natures until the pains and pleasures of others become ours also." That, surely, is an object worth seeking for, but it calls for patient effort and self-discipline.

We would all agree that a manhood without love and

imagination and humour would be sadly defective, and along with this we should remember the promise of our Christian calling that we may all attain to a full-grown man, to the measure of Christ's fulness (Eph. 4:13), for in Him Paul found the pattern of a complete manhood. Now our supposed purpose in the ministry is, by word and by life, to make Him visible. The preaching of One who, for our sakes, became poor, by men indolent and self-indulgent should always be recognized as an indecent anomaly. " It is not the Church which is the source of mischief," says Samuel Butler, " it is the Rectory," not the message but the bearer of it; so, for the prosperity of our work, we, whose imperfections abound, must get our vision cleared of what our Lord, in His perfection, was like, and then strive to imitate Him.

To the picture of Jesus in His work which we have considered in The Epistle to the Hebrews I must add a few notes of what Paul and the Gospels supply. In II Cor. 10:1 Paul appeals to his friends in name of " the meekness and considerateness of Christ," human graces of which they clearly all had heard as conspicuous in Him. The word ἐπιείκεια (considerateness) was familiar in Greek ethics: it is explained by Aristotle as the virtue of one who does not push his claim to extremes, but can make allowances, and is not a pedant for mere legality. It is closely akin to what we call equity, but this is possible only on the basis of a full understanding of what has been done, and why. Paul exalts this as peculiarly characteristic of Jesus, who knows us so well as to be able to judge aright of what we do. This is what we found so grotesquely absent in Augustine in his denouncing of a bunch of boys in a pear tree; and if we are worthily to exhibit Jesus we must resolutely follow the understanding master and not the vociferous servant. For another example of what Paul found most deeply characteristic of " the man Christ Jesus," I may refer to Phil. 1:8, where he protests that he yearns after them " in the heart of Christ " (ἐν σπλάγχνοις χριστοῦ). Paul himself was a great lover, with a nature so spacious and so hospitable that, as he travelled on from city to city, the circle of his unforgotten friends was always widening, yet he felt that this so ready love of his was only a pale reflection and derivative of the love of Christ. So he says, I yearn after you, but it is in the heart of Christ, who loved you before I did and who, if I could cease to care, would go on loving. His love embraces mine and inspires it: it is higher than mine, and it reaches down deeper, and it never fails. That is the love which carries men out beyond their own conditions into the lives and needs of others; and our work can only be done if we deliberately seek for more and yet more of the mind of Christ.

Two or three instances from the Gospels of the completeness of Christ's manhood must suffice. And first I would speak of the lordly authority which He exercised in His dealing with offenders. He knew men, and therefore He was bold in forgiving them. The often questioned French maxim — " *tout comprendre est tout pardonner* " — " to understand everything is to forgive everything " was more widely true of Him than of any other. In the two familiar stories of the adulterous woman (John 8:1–11) and the woman who was a sinner (Luke 7:37–50) the contrast between His way and ours is thrust upon us: the bystanders had nothing for these scandalous offenders but disgust and condemnation, whilst Jesus, looking more deeply, spoke only of hope and a new life of purity. There is another story much less familiar, because it has failed to keep the place it once had in Luke's Gospel (after Ch. 6:5), in which this boldness of His is still more startling: " On the same day when He saw a man working on the Sabbath Jesus said to him — ' Man, if thou knowest what thou art doing thou art blessed, but if thou knowest not thou art accursed and a transgressor of the law.' " In its sound the saying is so revolutionary that it is not surprising it was finally omitted from the Gospel. The teaching of it is repeated by Paul in Romans (Ch. 14:5, 6), — " One man reckons one day above another, whilst his neighbour reckons every day alike: let each be fully persuaded in his own mind. He who observes the day observes it to the Lord, and it is to the Lord that his neighbour does not observe it." On the surface, the man seemed plainly at fault, a transgressor and a rebel, and if he was merely preferring his own convenience and advantage to what he believed to be the will of God, he certainly was in revolt. But Jesus, looking more deeply, as Paul afterwards came to do, saw that a good man may recognize every day alike as God's day, and, with clear conscience, may do what a stricter legalist would reckon an offence. What appears in all these incidents is a man's gift of imaginative insight exercised courageously, which is not beyond the possibility of our imitation. He saw the facts, but He saw them lovingly, and thus His judgments were so full of hope.

Again in the Synoptics we are continually reminded of

the *tenderness* of Jesus. Mark, whose Gospel is so rich in touches taken from an eyewitness, twice over uses about Jesus an uncommon but delightful word to describe His handling of little children — a relation in which most of us are too self-conscious to appear to advantage: " He took them in the crook of His arm," says Mark (Mark 9:36; 10:16). That is what our Lord Jesus was like, " in the measure of His fulness." Again we may note how all the Synoptics, but only they, repeatedly use a word which they apply only to Jesus, as if He alone satisfied its emotional fulness — σπλαγχνίζεσθαι, to be deeply moved, to be touched to the heart. Jesus was thus affected, as we read, on the most diverse occasions: when He faced the tired and hungry crowd, when He faced a leper in his living death, when He listened to a father pleading for his epileptic boy — ἐσπλαγχνίσθη, He was passionately moved. That speaks of an emotion not to be mistaken, which we must possess if we are fully to exhibit Him to our fellows.

Gentlemen, if by any means we could attain to a complete manhood and the spirit of the mere official be extirpated in us, the quality of our ministry and the whole colour of our preaching would be changed: but such results are secured not by wishing for them, nor even by praying for them, but by deliberate and conscious effort as well to show forth the mind of Christ in His understanding of men and His eager will to help. It is thus that "the beauty of the Lord" may come upon us and that our work may be established by Him (Ps. 90:17).

THE ENRICHING OF A PREACHER
THROUGH READING

~

WHEN Milton had counselled his brother poets to ask God for that inspiration which can only come from above, he continued, "To this must be added industrious and select reading," a precept calling for special consideration from us, since the mind of a working minister is in constant danger of suffering, like soil relentlessly overcropped, where too much is taken out of the land and too little is put in.

I shall begin with one possible debt to reading which is too readily neglected. Men protest that, though they have no skill in decoration, they need not worry about style, since they can always make themselves understood. Perhaps they can: but Principal Denney, that master of lucid utterance, complained of his students that " not one man in a score of them can say just what he means, or put his meaning plainly down on paper." No doubt that ungifted race of students has long since disappeared, but such a lament from such a man might well awaken distrust in us, and set us considering how much we might gain by a surer mastery of words. I have no wish to distract your minds from your subject to mere considerations of style; my sole desire for each of you is that he should write as one who knows what he has to say and can say it shortly,

in living words however homely; for words do count, and
one is not as good as another. Words are living creatures,
having hands and feet, so that they can pursue and arrest.
During the horrors of the Crimean War, John Bright in
speaking of a House of Commons ready to sneer at a
Quaker's sermonizing, said, " The Angel of Death is very
near us, we can almost hear the beating of his wings," and
he admitted later that the one grave word " beating "
saved the whole effect of the passage. At the outbreak of
the present war we were informed, on the authority of
Whitehall, that the siren has a *warbling* note, as if it were
a thrush or a canary, as ludicrous an attempt at description as our language could furnish. By and by, our Prime
Minister, who has the useful habit of noting what things
are like and the gift of finding words to match them,
dubbed the siren a " banshee howling," and people confessed that at least the quality of the atrocity had been ex-
pressed. Now that is the secret of style: to keep your eye
on the object, to see what it is like, and then to attach
to it the fitting word. At a recent conference in Edinburgh, in prospect of a combined mission, the Chairman
urged that all the preparations should be " steeped in
prayer " — a pious though unarresting phrase; but he was
followed by an elder who said, " Aye, Mr. Chairman, and
we need to mind that a saut herrin' needs a *heap* o'
steepin'." That lighted up a commonplace with a sparkle
of humour, and secured it of being remembered, but it
also set people thinking that perhaps in some of the
Churches concerned forces unfriendly to revival had,
through years, been worked into their very substance, and
that these could only be got rid of now by a deliberate

and patient process. An apt word, whether it be a scholar's word or no, is a living power, whereas a string of customary verbiage is nothing but a strong soporific.

We should always think of our preaching as one particular kind of translation. It is not merely the Greek and Hebrew words in the Bible which are strange, but the manners and customs, the images employed, the standards acknowledged; and our task is to present the Bible message in such a way as to secure from our contemporaries an intelligent and a rejoicing welcome. Now, as we know, it is not enough for a translator to set down the dry, dictionary sense of the original words; he must try to reproduce something of their beauty and their splendour, which is never easy. Heine grumbled that his own songs, in a bad English rendering, were made to look " like moonbeams wrapped in straw," the dainty things quite ruined by their setting; and in our translation of God's message outrages of the same kind are continually committed. " The word of God is living and energetic and sharper than a sword," it is a flashing weapon of offence; but as we present it it may be as obsolete as Mons Meg, a lumbering memorial of a distant age. This is partly due to our unnatural pulpit voice, for, as Spurgeon once said to students, if they asked for a cup of tea " in such silly tones " as they used in preaching no one would dream that they seriously wished it. But even more of our failure is due to our slovenly, conventional phrasing, without simplicity and vital urgency. " I use market language," said Whitefield of his own preaching: the words must be plain and unmistakable in their meaning. But, as I have hinted, something more is required; we must try to do justice to the beauty of the message. In the synagogue at Nazareth the listeners " marvelled at the words of charm which came from Jesus' lips " (Luke 4:22): Mark reports (Mark 12:37) that " the mass of the people listened to Him with delight " (ἡδέως), and John tells (John 7:46) that even the officers sent to apprehend Jesus returned without their prisoner, saying, " No one ever spoke like this man." The Gospel is a very lovely thing, and we should take all possible pains to express it fittingly. When I insist on this I would have you remember that success in it is secured not by the use of painted words but by an interior glow of spirit in the preacher when he talks of the things of God as if, in Bunyan's words, " joy did make him speak."

Now there is no better way for the amending of our speaking than the eager study of right books. Your work now and in coming days may never give you wide spaces for reading, so you must husband what leisure you have: what Milton asked for is " industrious and *select* reading," and Coleridge would even narrow our range of *necessary* books to one. " Intense study of the Bible," he says, " will keep any writer from being vulgar in point of style," — just the Bible and apparently in King James's version, but the Bible *studied intensely*, which makes all the difference. Some of our very greatest preachers, without any pretensions to literature, have in this school alone learned the power and the majesty of words. But for this purpose of enriching and vitalizing our vocabulary, the Bible is not the only possible model: there is Bunyan, with his vivid, gripping sense of phrase, or even Burns, especially when he sticks to his Scots, might teach us the use of living words, without fumbling or repetition. In fact any book will serve in which the master rule has been followed of keeping one's eye on the object and declaring it in fit words.

But this vitalizing language is not the chief advantage secured by wise reading, it ought also to enlarge our whole outlook on the world. Most of us are sadly dim-sighted, and though the world is said to be the living garment of God and glorious in its variety, we often find it disappointingly monotonous and drab. Now Browning bluntly says that

> ". . . Art was given for that;
> God uses us to help each other so,
> Lending our minds out."

In our English version the prophets are referred to by Isaiah (Isa. 29:18) as the people's " eyes," the men who saw in a generation of the blind, and the worst calamity, in his view, which could befall his nation was that these " eyes " should be covered. You hope one day to stand as guides to your fellows, and you owe it to them as a duty that you should ever be on the alert for fresh discoveries of the wonder of life, which, from any quarter, may reach you. " This world's no blot for us nor blank, it means intensely and means good," and books are one special means for us of becoming aware of this. So A. B. Davidson maintained to his students that " all good literature is the most profitable study for the preacher, since in it the human mind is to be seen in all the breadth of its humanity — its emotions and aspirations and idealisms, its griefs and cries over failure." This demand need not scare

even a hard-driven minister. Ninety years ago a lad newly
licensed consulted his shrewd old minister as to books indispensable in his calling, and was told that there were
only two — " the Bible and Shakespeare: the one tells you
all you can know about God, and the other all you need
to know about man." We do not need to drive our lim-
itation quite so far, but the purport of the advice is evi-
dent: it is not the number but the quality of the books
which matters, and the way in which you use them. On
the shelves of most ministers there is a melancholy proportion of what Charles Lamb called βιβλια ἀβιβλα —
books not worth calling books, as they contribute nothing to our understanding of the gift of life. It is obvious
that books alone can never serve as a substitute for familiar intercourse with men and women: yet, like specta-
cles, they can help us in seeing more of the amazing variety of those whom we wish to guide and quicken — the
touches of splendour in them and their tragic relapses
into the mire. Life is infinitely various, just as the Bible
itself is: as Andrew Fairservice said, " There are mony
things ower guid for bannin' and ower bad for blessin',
like Rob Roy "; and if in our preaching we hold to the
few notes suggested by our laziness or our narrowness, we
shall do cruel injustice to our great theme. When a sentimental optimist bleated to Frederick the Great about the
natural goodness of men, the cynic King retorted, " *Er
kennt die verdammte Rasse nicht* " — " You do not know
the cursed race," and preaching with the opposite bias is
no less ineffective. I once knew a loud-voiced minister in
a slum district who loved to mount his pulpit, as Burns
says, " wi' tidings o' damnation," and, after addressing a

meeting in his parish, I asked a loafer standing by if he often came to the services. " No," he said, " when that man preaches in the Court here, bits come in at the window, but they're a' aboot hell and damnation, and we're sae weel acquent wi' thae words in the hoose that we dinna heed them much." That is one penalty for ignoring what Paul calls " the many-coloured wisdom of God," as it may come to us through the ministry of books.

But far beyond this richer understanding of life there is an inspiration which may come through reading. Much of the dullness of our preaching is due to the fact that it is the product of a jaded spirit. Ministers have generally too many sermons to prepare, and their work must often be done when they are tired and stupid, whilst others have too little to do and lethargy invades, with the result that men continually attempt the prophet's task without a touch of the prophet's furnishing. It is our main business to kindle in our people that faith which is the poetry of a common man's life: it lifts him above the tyranny of circumstance and makes him free of the ampler world of God, for it is not only saints who can sometimes " mount up with wings like eagles." But we who are commissioned thus to help our fellows are often ourselves bound among flats and fogs. I cannot stay to enlarge on how true prayer may achieve victories over the extremist lethargy of spirit; but a wise man will catch at anything which can set his mind and spirit in motion, as a noble book can do. Emerson claimed for his books, that, like the breeze, " they set the sails of my windmill spinning," a service which anyone might welcome.

All literature has been divided by De Quincey into two

groups — the books of knowledge and the books of power, the books which inform and those which move or inspire. He admits that from *Paradise Lost* you may derive no useful information, whereas in a cookery book you could learn something from every paragraph. "What you may owe to Milton is power, an expansion of your sympathy with the infinite, an assent as on a Jacob's ladder to heights above the earth, into an element where earth may be forgotten." Now if that is a fair description of what a living book may achieve in a sensitive spirit, could anything be imagined more to be coveted by us? In praise of his master Coleridge, Hazlitt confesses that when he might have gone all his days on his belly, like a snake in the dust: the great man had brought him to his feet and given him a share in higher things. That is our continual need as preachers — the expansion of our spiritual nature, without which our work sinks and becomes an earthbound drudgery.

Amongst the books of power, the Bible, which is " living and energetic," stands first beyond comparison. Augustine in his *Confessions* describes the long-continued gropings and desirings which brought him nothing, since he was suffering from a divided will — that too familiar " sickness of the mind"; but one day, as he reports, he opened the volume of Paul's Epistles and read where his eyes first alighted: " Not in rioting and drunkenness, not in chambering and wantonness, not in strife and envying; but put ye on the Lord Jesus Christ and make no provision for the flesh " (Rom. 13:13). " As I reached the end of the sentence the light of peace seemed to be shed upon my heart, and every shadow of doubt melted away." That is an instance representative of millions of what a book may do, how in a man it may at once imprison all meaner workings and cravings and release in him new powers of life. Augustine was in a single hour raised out of the slough of irresolution in which he was bogged: he learned the meaning of the word conversion, and this came to him from a book.

But it is not only in such fundamental effects that books have shown their power. Emerson, as we have seen, declared that they set his mind working; Mark Rutherfurd confesses that the reading of Wordsworth " recreated for him his Supreme Divinity, substituting a living Spirit for a Deity which had hardened into an idol "; and there are witnesses without end to the vastness and variety of men's debt to books. It is recorded of Keats that, in his twenty-second year, his mind and imagination all at once " became aflame with Shakespeare." The music of the poet's lines haunted him, but, what is more, they exalted and enriched and consoled him. When faced by extreme discouragement he says in a letter, " I never quite despair, and I read Shakespeare "; another day he writes, " This morning I felt lonely at breakfast, so I unboxed a volume of Shakespeare, for there is my comfort." And more broadly he says, " When a man has arrived at a certain ripeness of intellect, any grand and spiritual passage may serve him as a starting-post for all the two and thirty palaces " — away from the meanness and the worries and the threats of life out to a wide and glorious world. Gentlemen, is there not something of promise there for us in our most jaded moods? Keats was a great genius, and his response to the appeal of a book was inevitably prompter and more passionate than ours; but if even he, with his sensitive spirit, confessed such need of stimulation, how much more must we in our dullness! We should catch at anything which gives promise of leading us out into the spacious kingdoms of emotion and amazement and delight.

In search of this kind of inspiration we preachers should often turn to some of the so-called " Devotional Classics " — a group very vaguely defined, but whose uniting bond is a certain intensity of concentration upon God and His thoughts and ways. In one of his short poems Faber describes an " old labourer " who seemed to " find some jubilee in thinking " —

> " For his one thought was God,
> In that one thought he abode,
> For ever in that thought more deeply sinking — "

which is clearly the character of these outstanding books. In this country when the Devotional Classics are mentioned people are likely first to think of Augustine's *Confessions*, and à Kempis, and Pascal's *Thoughts*, and Bunyan's *Pilgrim* or *Grace Abounding*, with William Law, and Rutherfurd's *Letters*, and Faber, and Christina Rossetti lying close to the edge. My advice to you is to maintain a continuous intimacy with such books, but never to be overawed into professing an admiration and a debt which you do not feel, simply because admiration is customary. If, after trial, you find that a book has nothing for you, you should admit the fact and turn elsewhere. Even our beloved Paul allowed that there were people to whom he was not an apostle. Certainly my own passage through life has been marked in this by much of vagrancy and by a good many successive discoveries. My father was a devout Highland evangelical, with an eager dislike and distrust for Romanism, but amongst his books I found Faber's *Growth in Holiness,* closely and lovingly marked by him; and encouraged by that great book I read more and more of Faber's volumes, whose raptures of devotion made me, I think, a little less shy of giving a place to emotion in preaching. When I first came upon *The Little Flowers of St. Francis,* that miracle of the popular piety of the fourteenth century, the delight of the story captured me, and for months together the spirit of it seemed to stir life in my spirit. When I was a Glasgow minister Pascal began to take hold of me, that mightiest of them all. Others had their periods of contribution, longer or shorter — George Macdonald and Rendel Harris, that inspiring saint Christina Rossetti and many more — in helping the inner fires to glow. I think every man of us should have some such record of discovery and of debt, and the ministry of the new generation would be greatly less commonplace than ours has been if its preachers would learn, in Bacon's phrase, to " chew and digest " the writings of such God-intoxicated men. I have already warned you not to allow yourselves to be bludgeoned by mere authority into professing reverence for a book, because it is the fashion to admire it, though actually it adds nothing to you. Such imitative admiration is never enriching. And my other warning is: if you do admire and profit, do it with discrimination, for even a golden book is not all of it gold.

Take the most conspicuous example: any lover of the Synoptic Gospels must be conscious of one grave defect in *The Imitation of Christ,* marvellous and moving as it is.

Dean Milman bluntly says that " there never was a mis-
nomer so glaring as the title of this book," for it is too in-
active, too self-engrossed, too monkish at all to exhibit
the true character of Him " who went about doing good."
The author confessed that his delight was to sit " *in an-
gello cum libello* — in a corner with a book," in undis-
turbed enjoyment of his own holy thoughts, secluded not
only from the cares and sins of the world but from its duties. This ought never to be regarded as an imitation of
Christ, and yet what a medicine the book has been to agi-
tated souls, unbelieving almost as much as believing! In
spite of certain defects of the surface there is something
infinitely moving in Samuel Rutherfurd, of whom it was
said that " like a fish in the sea, he was never in his element but when he was commending his Lord," and who
could himself declare, when the Government had forbid-
den him to preach, " I had only one eye, and they have
put it out! " And yet, as Dr. Taylor Innes shrewdly notes,
Rutherfurd was really " a monk in a Scottish manse," he
never put himself in the place of others, but poured out
his own feelings as if these must be shared by any who
knew God. He was twice married and had nine children,
yet in the *Letters*, as Innes remarks, " we hear more of the
birds that built on Anwoth Kirk than of the bairns who
played in the Manse." This marks a startling contrast
with Luther in the point of humanity, and to this extent
the book is extravagant and apart from real life. Or if we
look dispassionately at *Grace Abounding* we find a book
so overcharged with introspection as to warrant its description as a sick book, a pathological record. Our merciful Father never meant us to keep company with our-

selves so much as Bunyan and his school did, nor has He made the way of return to Him so tangled and obstructed as Bunyan found it. Supreme as he was in his preaching, he had not learned in fulness Luther's lesson that " faith is a rejoicing confidence that we have a merciful God." But when this is noted, what glorious, heart-warming stuff the book contains about the wonder of God's patience and the boundlessness of His grace! If its vital substance were digested into our nature it would go far to reinstate in the vocabulary of our preaching that half-forgotten word — Salvation.

But though you read with discrimination, not swallowing books whole, or making them throughout a standard of religious life, you should not suffer this to dull your sense of admiration. Law's *Serious Call to a Devout and Holy Life*, even if it were nothing else, is a brilliant book: Gibbon, the historian, who had no love for piety, speaks of Law, whom he knew well, as " a saint and a wit." His object in writing, as indeed his chosen title suggests, was to provoke easy-going Christians to make their life match their professed belief, and it may be doubted if any religious book has proved more effective in the lives of famous men. Charles Wesley testifies that his views and feelings were wholly altered by it, and his brother John confesses that for three years he preached entirely after its model. George Whitefield, that blazing evangelist, reports that " God worked powerfully on my soul through that excellent treatise." When Johnson was an undergraduate, he took it up one day " expecting to find it a dull book, as such books generally are; but I found Law an overmatch for me, and this was the first occasion of my thinking in earnest." The evangelical commentator Thomas Scott, of whom Newman speaks as " the writer to whom I owed my soul," dated the beginning of his own spiritual life from the hour when he took up Law's book, " which hitherto I had treated with contempt." It is an astonishing record of power, all the more astonishing as Law was not distinctively an evangelical teacher. As Canon Overton puts it, " He set the ball a-rolling, though he did not care to follow it in its course." Yet, as we see, even in face of prejudice and contempt, like Johnson's and Scott's, the book has proved itself to be alive and a power of life in others.

And what shall I say in commendation of Pascal's *Thoughts*, the greatest and most purely original, as I reckon, of all the works which I have mentioned? It is not a book at all, but scattered notes in preparation for a book never written and not even outlined; yet in it, as nowhere else, I find the tangle and the tragedy of the human heart exposed and the glorious majesty of the God who redeems. " Man is only a reed," says Pascal, " but he is a reed that thinks. The great universe needs not to take up arms for his defeat, a drop of water or a poisoned vapour is enough for that: yet even if all its forces were mustered, man would remain nobler than the universe, for he knows that he is dying whilst it knows nothing." " Our human miseries are just so many proofs of man's greatness, for what is nature in a beast is utter degradation in a man. Ours are the miseries of a king who has lost his throne." " A man's heart is so spacious that it cannot be satisfied except with something of its own magnitude, and those indeed are happy who have found an object which does

them no dishonour, and which brings them salvation."
When he speaks of God it is in the same great tones. We
can never forget Augustine's sublime saying, " Thou hast
made us for Thyself, and our heart is restless until it rests
in Thee," but alongside of it we may boldly set the voice
which Pascal heard in his heart, " Be of good comfort,
thou wouldst not be seeking me, if thou hadst not already
found me." Even our cravings and disquiets are already
an evidence that the Spirit of the Father is at work, drawing His children home, or, as Cromwell so nobly put it,
" To be a Seeker is to be of the best sect next to the find-
ers; and such shall every faithful, humble seeker be at the
end." In the fourth Gospel two commands of Jesus appear which seem to clash: " Touch me not, for I am not
yet ascended," was His charge to Mary, whilst to Thomas
He said, " Reach hither thy hand and thrust it into my
side." But the apparent contradiction is relieved by Pascal in the glorious, evangelical saying, " It is only *in His
wounds* that the Risen Lord may be touched." And to
sum up all he declares, " If the mercy of God is so great
as to bring us salvation when He is only half disclosed,
what blaze of brightness must we look for when we see
Him as He is! "

Gentlemen, it is with books like these in which God is
first and last that I would have you make acquaintance,
for the loving study of them would set the heart vibrating
with wonder, love and praise. Such reading would give
substance and majesty to our preaching, and enable us to
indulge sometimes in that lyric note which so well becomes the man who proclaims " the Gospel of the *glory*
of the Blessed God."

THE THEME AND QUALITY OF
THE PREACHING WHICH SHOULD ENSUE

I HAVE spoken of the making of a preacher — of things indispensable for him and of things desirable, so now I wish to talk of the preaching which ought to ensue: what of its substance? and what of its tone? What Shakespeare exalts in his ideal minister is the man's entire fidelity to the message of God:

> "Who hath not heard it spoken
> How deep you were within the books of God?
> To us the speaker in His parliament,
> To us the imagined voice of God Himself:
> The very opener and intelligencer
> Between the grace, the sanctities of Heaven
> And our dull workings."

This matches closely with Malachi's ideal (Mal. 2:2) that "the priest's lips should keep knowledge, and men should seek instruction at his mouth, for he is the messenger of the Lord of Hosts." Knowledge of God's mind and fidelity in declaring it — these would seem to be the two essentials. Bunyan depicts the minister of his choice as a man "with the world behind his back, with the law of truth upon his lips, who stands as if he pleaded with men": that is the preacher as he ought to be, in character, subject and attitude, the kind of man he is, the theme which engages him, and the mood in which he deals with it.

Such ideals are unfortunately too seldom realized in practice. The Dean of St. Paul's recently declared that " the Church seems to be losing hold both without and within," by which, I suppose, he meant that it appeals to a smaller proportion of our population than it did, and that it touches its own people in a more superficial way. For this loss of grip many causes might be alleged, but certainly the preaching cannot escape some share of the blame. Shakespeare suggests that a preacher should be " to us the imagined voice of God Himself," but this, as the Psalmist declares (Ps. 68:33), is " a mighty voice," so that all our trivialities and fripperies of decoration are ruled out. A minister of no striking gift, if he is always concerned with the mighty acts of God, and speaks of these as best he can, will never wholly fail, whereas a vastly cleverer man may achieve nothing of account. Some years ago a volume of sermons was issued, and sold well and gained applause; but that wise man Dr. Henderson of Crieff remarked to me upon it, " Does the fellow not know that there is anything *great* in the New Testament? " And the same condemnation is deserved by many.

In these lectures I have insisted on two things as indispensable for a preacher — a personal knowledge of God and a knowledge of men and their ways, from each of which, as it seems to me, a guiding rule or standard for preaching may be derived. On the one hand, we must aim in our pulpit work at harmony with the magnificence and the mercy of God, and on the other hand, our preaching must match the needs of a creature so many-sided as man, and especially, it must never by any kind of triviality mock man's dire necessities. It is fitting that on these two primary demands I should enlarge.

1. Any preacher who has a real acquaintance with God must desire to let others know what that God is like. He accepts for himself the duty which Peter (I Peter 2:9) imposes on all Christians of " proclaiming the mighty deeds of Him who has called us into His marvellous light." This is a duty too often shirked by preachers. A witty English bishop complained of a sermon that " it did not contain Gospel enough to convert a tomtit," and we have been fortunate if we have not frequently heard discourses of this kind, which proclaimed nothing and aimed at nothing, and were a sheer irrelevance in the worship of a living and a mighty God.

Paul repeatedly calls the message which we are supposed to publish " The Gospel of God," i.e., the goodness which God has sent to the world. In due time this Gospel had been committed to Paul as a trust, so he bids his friends in Corinth (I Cor. 4:1, 2) think of him always as " a servant of Christ and a *steward* of the purposes of God." A steward is not free to do what he chooses with the resources put in his hands, but must give account of all he has done and not done, and the first requirement made of him is that he be faithful (I Cor. 4:2). So Paul again affirms (II Cor. 4:2; 2:17), " I have renounced everything that is underhand or disgraceful, and I do not adulterate [or play tricks with] the word of God." God's intention in entrusting him with this stewardship was that he should *fully preach* ($\pi\lambda\eta\rho\dot{\omega}\sigma\alpha\iota$) the word of God, for his relation to it was not that of a diplomatist who, by dexterous concessions, seeks for the best terms attainable: it was that of a herald sent to announce the sovereign mind and will of Almighty God. Thus the matter of our preaching seems to be prescribed, and we are guilty of something like a breach of trust if for this " Gospel of God " we substitute something of our own devising. Thus we come upon a first characteristic of right Christian preaching: if the preacher is faithfully discharging his commission his work will always bear some *note of authority*. Professor Archibald Duff in one place draws attention to an interesting change in the tone of Jewish preaching in the fifth and sixth centuries A.D. For a long time the Synagogue teachers had enjoyed the title of the *Amoraim* — the speakers — but now they preferred to be called the *Seboraim* — the holders of opinions. They no longer cared to announce, " God has said this or this "; they preferred timidly to murmur, " We think that such and such is probably the mind of God." In a multitude of details such modesty is commendable, but in the central and vital matters, in which God's mind is declared, it is of no avail. " That which overcometh the world is our faith," says John.

This lawful note of authority is something deeper than an idle confidence in one's own opinion or a habit of dogmatism. If a man in his own experience has made discoveries of the power and the mercy of God, and if these discoveries are confirmed from other lives and from the Scriptures, he has what Calvin called " the testimony of the Holy Spirit " to make him bold, and, like Paul, he can affirm, " This is a true word, fit everywhere to be received as true," it is a declaration which can stand scrutiny of the acts and powers of the Invisible God. But if this is its character how great a wrong is done when, in preaching, a mere Christian flavouring is added to a kettleful of innocuous chatter such as fills so many sermons! It is told of poor Louis XVI that, on coming out of church one day, he remarked to one of his attendants, " If the good Abbé had talked a little about religion to-day, I think he would have mentioned everything." I once heard a preacher of reputation in his church in London, and was entertained by a sufficiently clever performance. The one thing clear was that, like Chaucer's doctor of physic, the speaker's " study was but little on the Bible," for though the brief discourse was closely larded with quotations, mainly from Galsworthy, he never once quoted from Scripture. Many years ago an ardent admirer of one of our ministers took me to his church on a Communion Sunday, and at the close pressed for my opinion: I had to confess that the whole service struck me as a little wooden and unuplifting. " Ah," said my friend, " but you should hear him when he is at his best — on social questions: the other Sunday he was speaking about bad housing and drainage, and he was grand!" Gentlemen, if we have been put in trust with the Gospel of God, do you think it fitting or even honest that the balance of our message should be adjusted in a way like that? The only adequate comment on a preacher who reached the heights on the subject of drainage is that made to the artist Benjamin Haydon on his once famous picture of " Christ Entering Jerusalem ": the poet Samuel Rogers looked at it, and then, with gentle malice, remarked, " I think, Mr. Haydon, your ass is the saviour of the picture." In our preaching Christ should always have the central place that He first may catch and engage the attention of all. In a world of so many cares and tragedies we ought not to be of the hesitating Seboraim, but of those who, like John, can confidently declare, " We *know* that the Son of God has come and has given us insight to know Him that is true: and we are in Him that is true, even in His Son Jesus Christ, for He is the true God and the Life Eternal."

Next to this note of authority I would set a note of *expectation*: the word of God is in our mouth, and we ought constantly to expect that, since it is " living and energetic," it will do something. Preaching should never be abstract, but should bear directly on life. The words which Jesus announced at Nazareth as the programme of His ministry had all of them some practical effect in view: " The Lord has annointed me to bring good news to poor people, to proclaim release to captives and sight to the blind, to send the crushed on their way with troubles left behind them, and to announce that God's time for doing all this has arrived." Everything there, as you see, aims at result, and all right preaching should be set to that key, for it is characteristic of all God's speaking. " He spake and it was done," says one Psalmist: " the Word became flesh," says John, " and He dwelt among us full of grace and full of reality." Since God is the Creator, His thoughts should always be conceived of as on the way to becoming things, so whenever we preach His word it should always be with expectation, as on the edge of decisions and transformations, and we should never forget the stern saying of

Jesus (Matt. 12:36) that " for every idle word a man shall speak he must give account to God." Jesus did not say every false or evil word: the word used is ἀργὸν, which in Scots we may translate as *do-less,* a word on which no result could be expected to follow. Could there be an apter description or a graver condemnation of many of our feckless outpourings, without sufficient gospel in them to convert a tomtit?

But, if we know God, we must desire in our preaching to secure some more intimate *indication of His character,* who is not only a great God but a Saviour, and indeed no preaching can be true to either Testament which has not at its heart the announcement of a mighty deliverance. Paul describes his message as " the Gospel of the *glory* of the Blessed God," i.e., the Gospel in which the splendour of God most triumphantly appears, and to talk to men of anything without this, at least, as background would have seemed to him a wanton waste of time. We live in a world of unrest and frustration, a world " bursting with sin and sorrow," in which by our own effort we can have no security, but the very badness of our situation may encourage the assurance that He in whom is the fountain of all nobleness will certainly strike in as Saviour. George Adam Smith singles out " the three great protestations of prophecy," and sets as the last and mightiest of these the assertion that " God is not mere law or love at a distance, but that He strikes into our ethical warfare and passion." The older prophets had to grope and struggle towards such a conviction, but once it was attained it was hailed as the supreme of marvels; and both the Testaments ring with the proclamation of it. " In all their affliction He was afflicted, and the Angel of His presence saved them: in His love and in His pity He redeemed them." " Who is a God like unto Thee who pardoneth iniquity, who retaineth not His anger for ever because He delighteth in mercy? " The ancient hymns which Luke has introduced into his Gospel sound the same note of jubilation: " He hath visited and redeemed His people "; " Mine eyes have seen Thy salvation which Thou hast prepared to meet the need of every nation." In the book of The Acts we find that the centre of the early preaching was that " the Messiah was bound to suffer ": as Wellhausen says, that was " *the Christian credo*." The Galatians are reminded that Paul's preaching was all of it a " picturing " of Jesus Christ as crucified, for every doctrine he proclaimed and every duty he enforced had as its background and its spring that amazing coming down of Heaven to earth. The message of all Scripture is that Salvation belongeth unto God, and no one has ever begun to preach as he ought who does not give the central place to God as the Saviour.

2. And what has our knowledge of men to contribute to our preaching? The prophets and sages of the Old Testament were exasperated by the superficial diagnosis which was offered of our human hurt. " You are all physicians of no value," cries Job: " if you were wiser you would hold your peace." " They heal the hurt of the daughter of my people slightly," says Jeremiah, " saying Peace, Peace — it is all right — when there is no peace." Ezekiel derisively describes some preachers as setting up a slim wall of defence and daubing it with whitewash to make it look substantial, but " deluges of rain are coming,

with hail and a stormy blast, and your wall, in spite of the whitewash, will collapse." We have long been accustomed to hear that man is not tragically hurt, and that with better social conditions and more of education and encouragement in self-control the mischief can be corrected. Is it to this that our knowledge of men would lead? Are we also " physicians of no value "? In his Report to last Assembly Dr. John Baillie insisted that the doctrine of man is now the central area of conflict. For some generations it had too sanguinely been assumed that scientific progress would join hands with spiritual progress, and that together they would " proceed in a swiftly mounting curve." But the boasted advances in technology have got out of hand, and we have seen them actively threatening the destruction of the higher interests of the race; so now an opposite tide is setting in of disillusion and despair, a mood of cynical indifference and distrust of idealisms of every sort. It is obvious that neither of these moods is entirely new, for the eighteenth century had its share both of sentimental rhetoric about the goodness of the natural man, which provoked the great King's snarl, " *Er kennt die verdammte Rasse nicht*," and of the embittered gloom of Swift in his *Gulliver's Travels.* " I heartily hate and detest that animal called man," he said, " and on this basis of misanthropy the whole building of my Gulliver is erected"; and again, " If you expect no more from man than such an animal is capable of, you will every day find my description of the Yahoos truer to reality." Our present situation is not entirely new, but this does not make the need of a remedy less compelling. When such thoughts as I have quoted held Swift's mind it is not surprising to find him admitting that he "could only preach Pamphlets now," since nothing of the nature of Gospel was left to him. "It is through Jesus," says Peter (I Peter 1:21), "that we are believers in God," and that "our faith is also a hope in God." It is to Jesus and His thoughts of men that we must turn, if our hope for the world is to abide.

What are we then to say of these things? What is man, this baffling creature, so obtrusively two-natured, dust of the earth and breath of God? Many dogmatic statements about human depravity have been so exaggerated as to invite protest, for it is obvious that they are not true; yet the mystery and the contradiction remain:

> "I know my soul hath power to know all things, yet is she
>   blind and ignorant of all:
>   I know I'm one of Nature's little kings, yet to the least and
>   vilest things am thrall:
>   I know my life's a pain and but a span, I know my sense is
>   mocked in everything:
>   And, to conclude, I know I am a man, which is a proud and
>   yet a very wretched thing."

That is not unlike Pascal, though his Gospel is unexpressed. "Our very miseries are so many indications of our greatness — they are the miseries of a king who has lost his throne." It is thus that Jesus saw the life of men and women — kindly but also spaciously — and His example should constrain us in our preaching to exalt this conception of the magnificence of human nature and the magnitude of its disaster as the necessary background of our proclamation of a remedy. Disease and remedy condition one another; and if the trouble of men is superficially conceived, the need of an intervention utterly divine must be diminished and the spring of our final confidence broken. It is through Jesus that we believe in God and in the future of His world.

Thus both by our knowledge of God and our knowledge of men and their needs we are pushed in our preaching out to a region of mighty things — the greatness of man and the answering greatness of his disgrace and the surpassing greatness of the deliverance of God. And yet, even in an age so high and stirring as our own, there is in many quarters a bewildering fondness for what is trivial in preaching. Ninety years ago, when Dr. Dale was beginning his work in Birmingham, he was warned by a neighbour not to try to preach doctrine, that the people would not stand it. " They'll have to stand it," was his reply, for it was thus he conceived of the gravity of the ministry entrusted to him. I would that all of you might have a share in that sturdiness of spirit, for the rule given to Jeremiah (Jer. 15:19) for the guidance of his work applies not less to us: " Let them return to thee, but return not thou unto them."

I have spoken of certain notes in Christian preaching — authority and expectation and centrality of theme — but to these I would add another in which we often fail. Newman, that master in our craft, has laid it down that " *definiteness* is the life of preaching." A really live sermon has been described as " a speech concluding with a motion," and though this may not cover every case it must be admitted that something is lacking in a preacher who does not frequently compel his hearers to face decisions. As we read in Deuteronomy (Ch. 30:19) the preacher's characteristic note is, " I have this day set before you life and good or death and evil: therefore choose life, that thou and thy seed may live," or in modern fashion we have Browning's challenge,

> " It may be false, but would you wish it true?
> Has it your vote to be true if it may? "

Unfortunately definiteness of this kind is not in fashion, and it is always easier to shamble vaguely on, saying nothing in particular and aiming at no distinct result. It would be for our good if we all could lay to heart Paul's precept given to Timothy (II Tim. 4:2): " Preach the word in season and out of season: rebuke, convict, plead with your hearers: never lose patience with them, and never give up teaching."

In the special matter of teaching our task is enormously harder than our fathers' was, for the background of clear knowledge, both of doctrine and of Scripture, on which they could count in their people has largely disappeared. The Shorter Catechism, with its teaching about God and life, so spacious in conception, and so superbly lucid and concise in expression, has fallen out of use; and, what is much graver, the old familiarity with Scripture has gone. In my experience as professor few things struck me as more ominous than the bewildering ignorance of the Bible among our students, for, though a few really knew it, far more seemed to regard it only as a book to be got up for examination, and dismissed from memory as soon as the examination was over: to those it was in no way a familiar companion — a lamp to their feet and a light upon their path. In the book of The Proverbs (Ch. 6:22) we read of God's law that " when you are at work it will be your guide, when you lie down to sleep it will quiet your spirit, and in the morning when you rise it will talk to you of God ": that exactly describes what the Bible used to be to hosts of our plain people, but this loving familiarity has sadly diminished. The Head of one of our Universities once confessed to me his dismay in noting how centrally Christian terms, like faith and grace and salvation, seemed to have lost meaning for a mass of students, and were treated by them as mere scraps of empty, pulpit jargon. Ought there not, he asked, to be much more of systematic explanation of such terms to show how closely they touch on life? This need for definite instruction is increased to-day by the portentous development in our country of queer, fancy religions. From many districts reports have come of the disquieting success of one of them which, even three years ago, was able to boast that 309,000,000 of its publications, in more than seventy languages, had been distributed or sold. A student of theological eccentricities can scarcely help smiling at the variety of errors, ancient and modern, which have been tossed together into these witches' cauldrons — that the Divine Spirit withdrew from Jesus on the Cross, so that He died as mere man, that the soul is not immortal, that only 144,-000 persons will finally be found in " the Body of Christ," and so forth. But the Church is not wise simply to smile at so quaint a re-emergence of Gnostic and other ancient heresies; it has to ask why its simple people are so readily seduced: it is because they have not been taught. And the situation can be amended only by deliberate instruction in the evangelical faith, so that men may see not only that it is true, but that they may glory in holding to it.

This quality of definiteness is supremely necessary in our ethical preaching, because it is in that quarter that amongst our people we are apt to find most of misunderstanding and suspicion. On the one hand is the body of almost fanatical evangelicals, whose watchword is: " You must preach the Gospel, and not let yourself be drawn aside to play the part of a mere moralist. Certainly you should preach about sin, the sin whose ' wages is death ': you must exhibit this as a thing so hideous that nothing less than the sacrifice of the Son of God could suffice for its removal." In this you may heartily acquiesce, but ere long you may discover that people who have listened with approbation for half a lifetime to this theological denouncing of sin are not in the least conscious of their own meanness and worldliness and self-indulgence, since these are common in the society which they frequent. It has never occurred to them that it is sneaking, wee sins like theirs which brought our Lord Jesus most nearly to despair: about outcasts and harlots He had no difficulty, for they knew they were in fault, but the church-going pharisees and their friends, who plumed themselves on their virtue — they were the real problem. How are these people to be made to hear, unless, as Paul says, there be a preacher? The Confession of Faith, with more wisdom than these too suspicious evangelicals, bids us not content ourselves with "a general repentance, for it is every man's duty to repent of his particular sins particularly," so a faithful preacher will often strike at these particulars.

Another reason which makes definiteness in moral teaching essential is that so many of our people conceive of morality narrowly and superficially: do not do anything actively wrong — don't kill or steal or fornicate, and nothing more is required. You may derive your income from house property in such a condition as to threaten both health and decency, but if the public authority does not move, why should you worry? Arthur Hugh Clough ironically says to such people,

> " Thou shalt not kill, but needst not strive
> Officiously to keep alive:
> Thou shalt not steal, an empty feat
> When it's more lucrative to cheat."

People need deliberately to be taught that the New Testament requires us not merely to abstain from doing evil but actively to endeavour to do good: its rule is not negative, made up of prohibitions, it is positive. Paul (Eph. 4:28) is not content to bid a thief give up stealing; he adds, " Let him work at an honest trade that he may have to *give* to people in need." In dropping the Shorter Catechism out of use we are apt to forget this lesson which it so consistently presses home. The Sixth Commandment, as the Catechism understands it, requires " all lawful endeavours to preserve the life of others," and the Eighth requires not merely that we should not steal but that " in every lawful way we should procure and further the wealth and outward estate of others." There is ample room for definite teaching and example in this Christian view of morals.

In what has been called " *the preaching of conquest* "

— the preaching which directly aims at conversion — the need of definiteness is obvious. This noble kind of preaching is not every man's gift; Paul humbly claims that whilst to him some knack of " planting " had been given, to Apollos the secondary (though indispensable) gift of " watering " had been entrusted. An evangelist of renown in Birmingham confessed that many who came to him for conversion had had to pass on to his neighbour Dale " to be finished ": the two tasks are by no means always — perhaps not often in their perfection — in the same hands. And yet I would urge you not to abandon the hope of speaking the transforming, liberating word in human lives: never allow to yourself that you have no gift for evangelism, and need not try, for wonders still are wrought by the ungifted, and it still is true (Isa. 28:11) that " with stammering lips and another tongue God speaks to the people." If this is to be our happy experience we must practise definiteness in our address. Every evangelist must cultivate the power of isolating the individuals in front of him, so that the disturbing sense of a surrounding crowd is lost, and preacher and hearer, with God as witness, are shut in together. It is obvious that this means that we never talk obliquely in our sermons, of what *people* do or ought to do: it is not " a general repentance " at which we are aiming, and there we must speak as to the individual of his duty and his decision.

Rigorous dogmatists have sometimes been disquieted by the story of evangelism: they feel that Salvation and a new life can only come through the Gospel preached in their way, and yet stubbornly the facts are against them. George Whitefield, as a stout Calvinist, maintained for many years that Wesley, as an Arminian, preached "a different Gospel" from his, which it was his duty to expose and denounce; but during these years of strife they both were passing from victory to victory in their capturing of men. Even Dr. James Denney, in his *Studies in Theology*, exhibits the same combative and exclusive spirit: preachers who did not hold his express doctrine of expiation are dismissed by him as being, in Paul's words, "men in whom the Gospel is hid," and he compares them in their evangelism to witless fishers who go to the burnside with hooks without a barb. The bait may be taken, but no fish is ever caught. Now it may be true that one particular dogmatic form has proved itself the most readily effective in evangelistic preaching, but it does not follow that every other is excluded, for, as the Bible tells us, there are gates of entrance into the city of God from East and West, from North and South. Yet, on different occasions, when Henry Drummond was urged to extend to Glasgow his work amongst students in Edinburgh, opposition meetings were at once organized to combat the mischief which poor Drummond, with his looser dogmatic theories, might do. He of course withdrew, as he would not have the Gospel preached of contention, and thus a rich possibility of lasting good was lost to our University. Yet on both sides the sole desire was that Christ should be preached and lives be won for Him. Does it follow that definiteness in teaching is not required at all in the preaching of conquest, or only that many dogmatists carry their peculiarities too far? When Jesus (John 3:14) compared Himself to the brazen serpent He seemed to suggest that the one *indispensable* is that He should be lifted up and made conspicuous, so that sick and despairing eyes may see Him as the object of their hope. " In Him alone," as Calvin says, " is *tota materia salutis nostrae* — the whole stuff of our salvation." That might be accepted as the guiding principle of every evangelist: each may interpret, illustrate, enforce as his experience has taught him, but the centre and the substance are here. "I have only one sermon," said Hofacker, " Come, sinners, and look on Christ! and I have found that he who preaches Christ never runs alone." A comrade reported of Richard Cameron, the Covenanter in his ministry in the Killing Days, " The bias of his heart lay to the proposing of Christ and persuading men to close with him." Thus to exalt Him as the sole Hope and Redeemer of men is enough — strong amid the broken, erect among the fallen, living amid the dead and the dying, Jesus Christ, the Son of God, our Lord. It is thus the Gospel should always be preached, and thus rejoicingly it should be received.